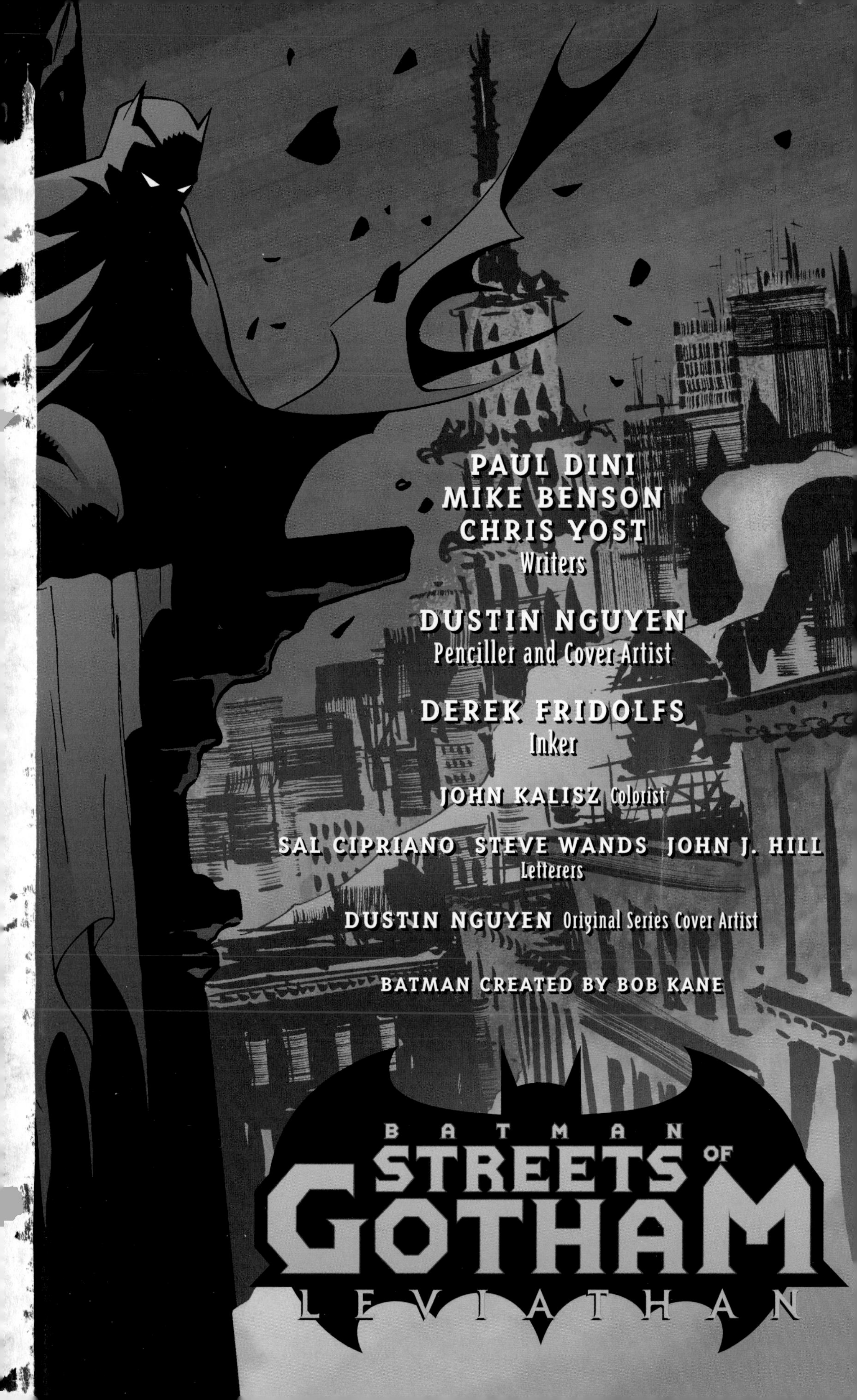

PAUL DINI
MIKE BENSON
CHRIS YOST
Writers

DUSTIN NGUYEN
Penciller and Cover Artist

DEREK FRIDOLFS
Inker

JOHN KALISZ Colorist

SAL CIPRIANO STEVE WANDS JOHN J. HILL
Letterers

DUSTIN NGUYEN Original Series Cover Artist

BATMAN CREATED BY BOB KANE

BATMAN STREETS OF GOTHAM
LEVIATHAN

Mike Marts
Editor — Original Series

Janelle Siegel
Assistant Editor — Original Series

Bob Harras
Group Editor — Collected Editions

Scott Nybakken
Editor

Robbin Brosterman
Design Director — Books

Curtis King Jr.
Senior Art Director

DC COMICS

Diane Nelson
President

Dan DiDio and Jim Lee
Co-Publishers

Geoff Johns
Chief Creative Officer

Patrick Caldon
EVP-Finance and Administration

John Rood
EVP-Sales, Marketing
and Business Development

Amy Genkins
SVP-Business and Legal Affairs

Steve Rotterdam
SVP-Sales and Marketing

John Cunningham
VP-Marketing

Terri Cunningham
VP-Managing Editor

Alison Gill
VP-Manufacturing

David Hyde
VP-Publicity

Sue Pohja
VP-Book Trade Sales

Alysse Soll
VP-Advertising and Custom Publishing

Bob Wayne
VP-Sales

Mark Chiarello
Art Director

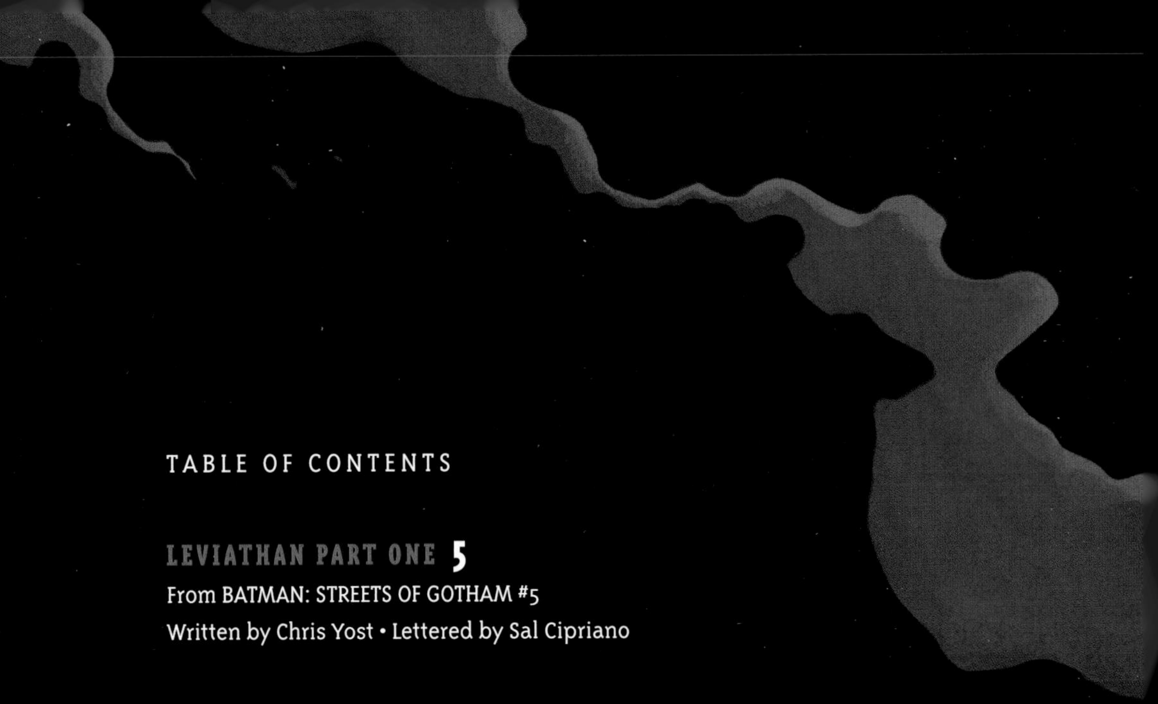

TABLE OF CONTENTS

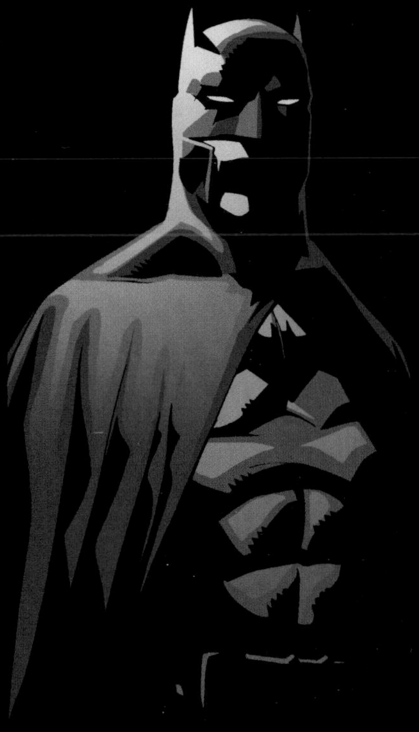

B A T M A N

REBORN

In the aftermath of the universe-shattering events
known as the Final Crisis, Gotham City's Dark Knight
is presumed dead.

With the mantle of the Bat unclaimed, a battle
erupts between Dick Grayson, the original Robin,
and his corrupted successor, Jason Todd — just as
the Black Mask destroys Arkham Asylum and
sets its inmates loose to wreak havoc upon the
vulnerable city.

In the resulting Battle for the Cowl, Dick Grayson is
joined by Bruce Wayne's son Damian, and together
they emerge victorious as a new and decidedly
different Batman and Robin.

Meanwhile, after assuming the identity of Red Robin,
former sidekick Tim Drake sets out on a quest that will
eventually take him around the world — a quest to
prove that the original Batman is still alive...

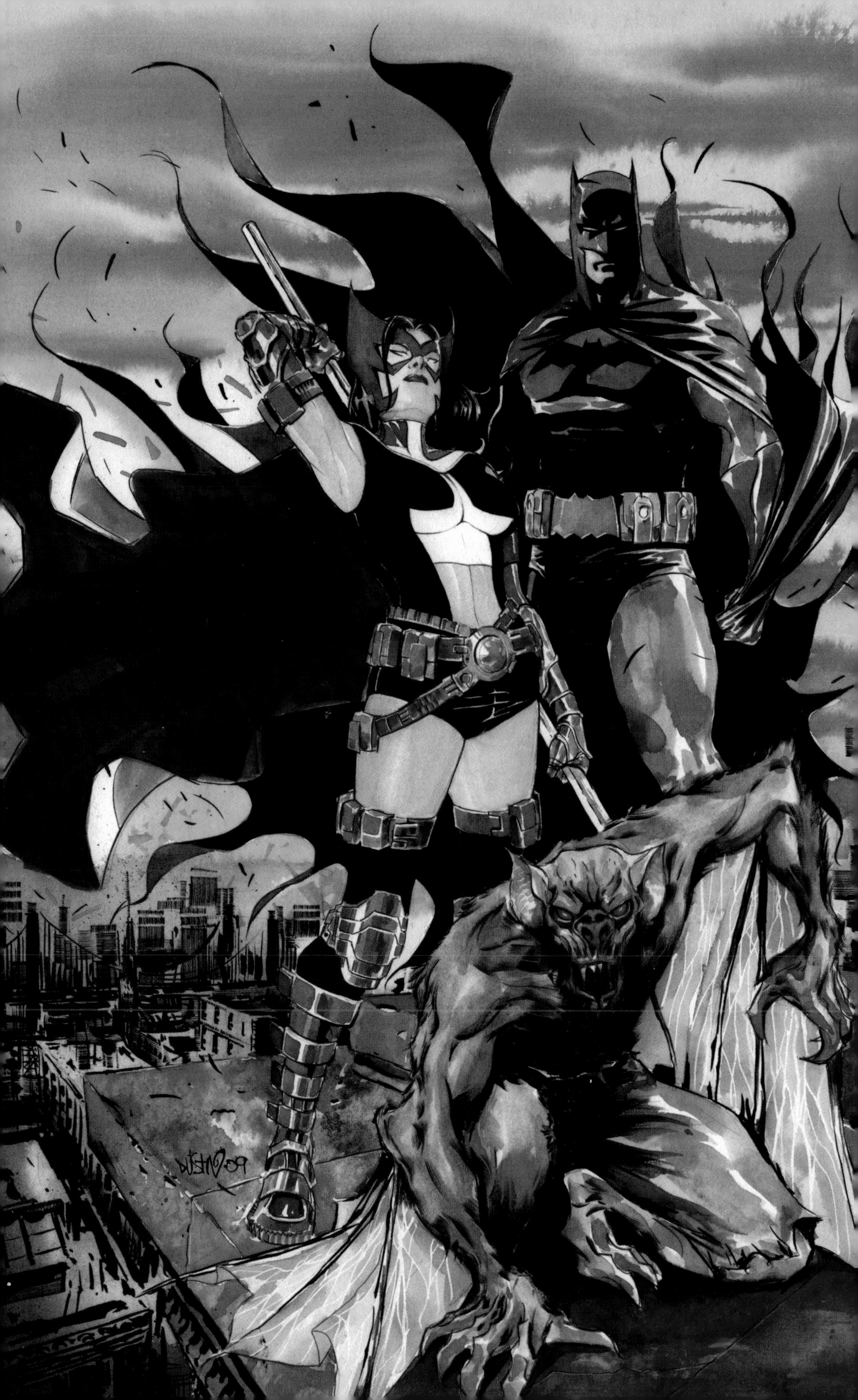

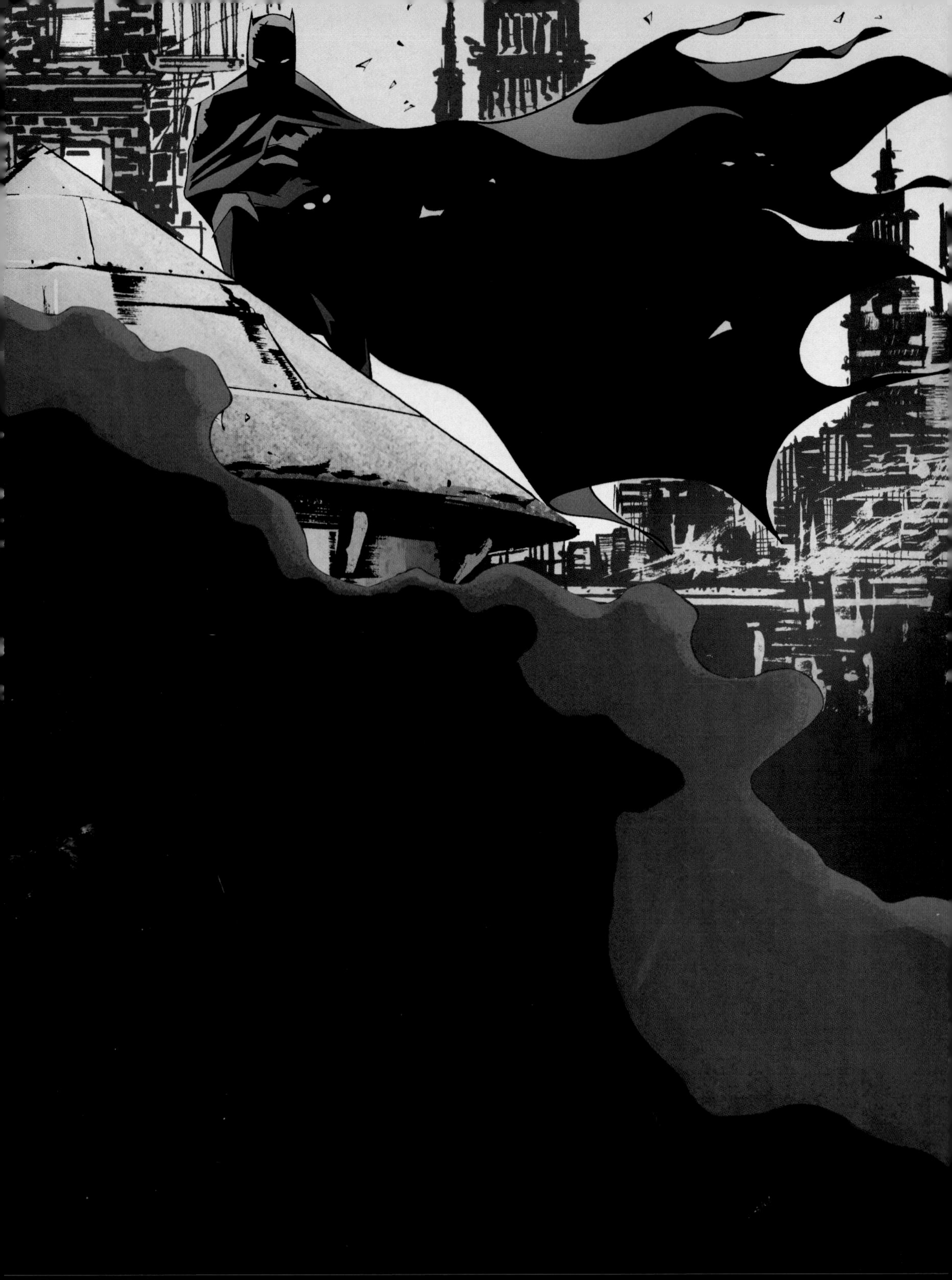

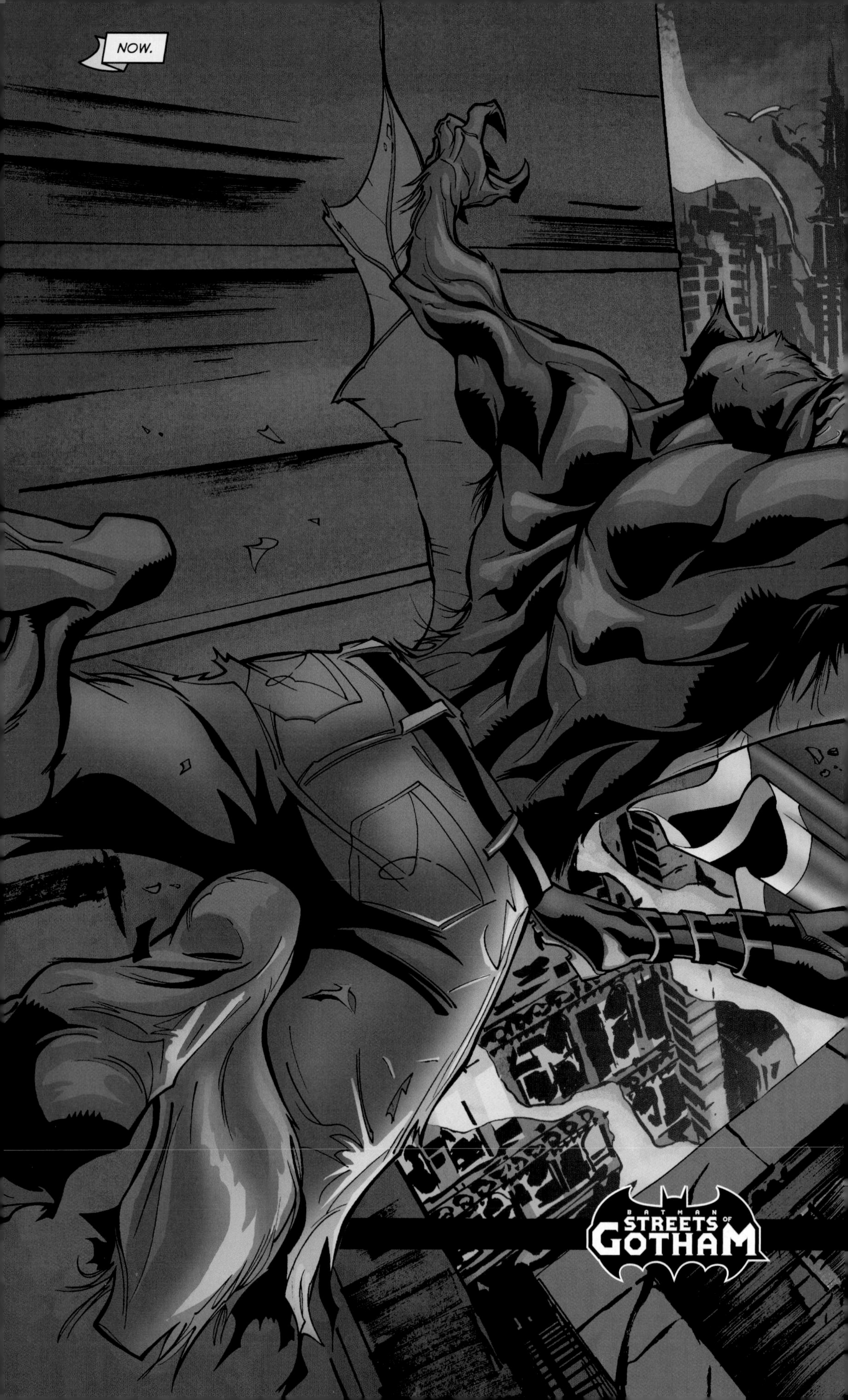
NOW.
BATMAN
STREETS OF
GOTHAM

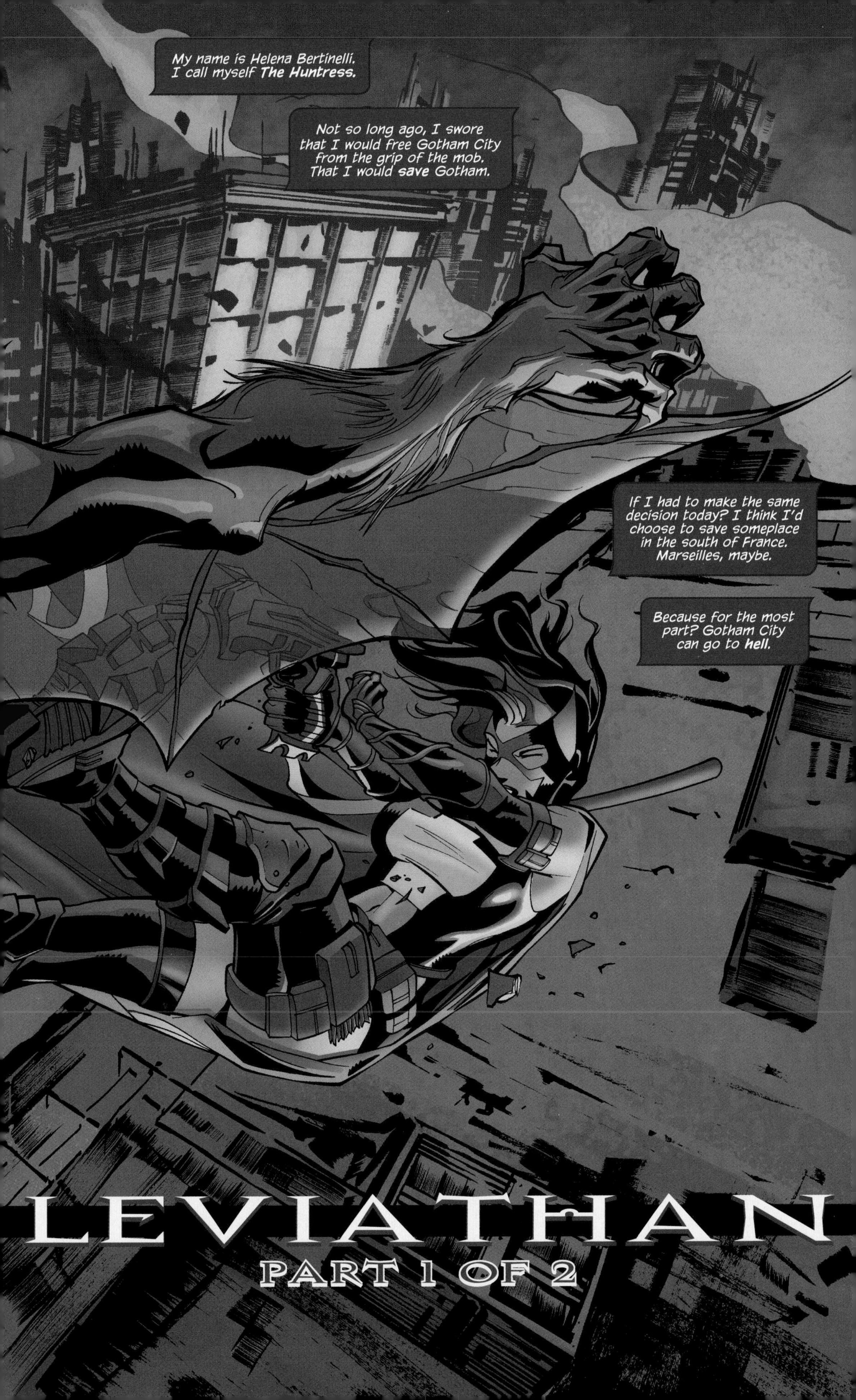

My name is Helena Bertinelli. I call myself The Huntress.
Not so long ago, I swore that I would free Gotham City from the grip of the mob. That I would save Gotham.
If I had to make the same decision today? I think I'd choose to save someplace in the south of France. Marseilles, maybe.
Because for the most part? Gotham City can go to hell.
LEVIATHAN
PART 1 OF 2

The giant monster trying to kill me? Kirk Langstrom, the Man-Bat.

SHUNK

SHUNK

UHN!

Why's he trying to eat me? No idea.

I fire wide, just to avoid the lectures. Oracle and Nightwing...

The irony is that Barbara told me that Langstrom was showing more self-control of late.

Supposedly he could even transform from man to Man-Bat and back again, without the serum he normally takes to initiate the change.

HT!

Not Nightwing. Batman.

Well, Oracle needs to update her files, because "control" isn't on the menu today.

Batman would get all upset at me for killing him, and I'd never hear the end of it.

WHUMP

Yet another case of Batman giving a monster a second chance.

If there's a man left inside there, I can't see it.

Jason Todd, Two-Face, Riddler...now this animal.

THAK

SKREEE

Sometimes with animals, you have to put them down.

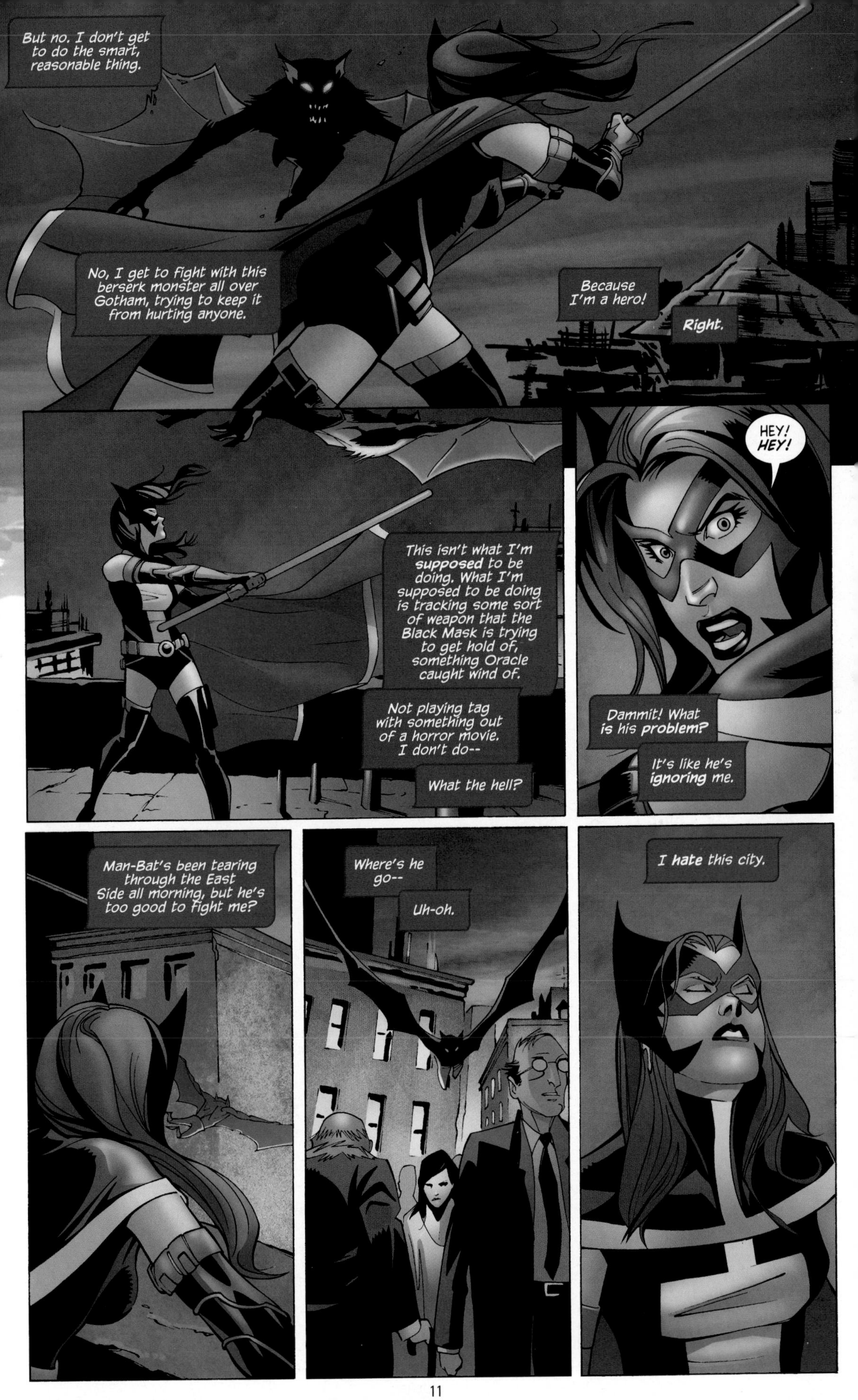

But no. I don't get to do the smart, reasonable thing.
No, I get to fight with this berserk monster all over Gotham, trying to keep it from hurting anyone.
Because I'm a hero!
Right.
This isn't what I'm supposed to be doing. What I'm supposed to be doing is tracking some sort of weapon that the Black Mask is trying to get hold of, something Oracle caught wind of.
Not playing tag with something out of a horror movie. I don't do--
What the hell?
HEY! HEY!
Dammit! What is his problem?
It's like he's ignoring me.
Man-Bat's been tearing through the East Side all morning, but he's too good to fight me?
Where's he go--
Uh-oh.
I hate this city.

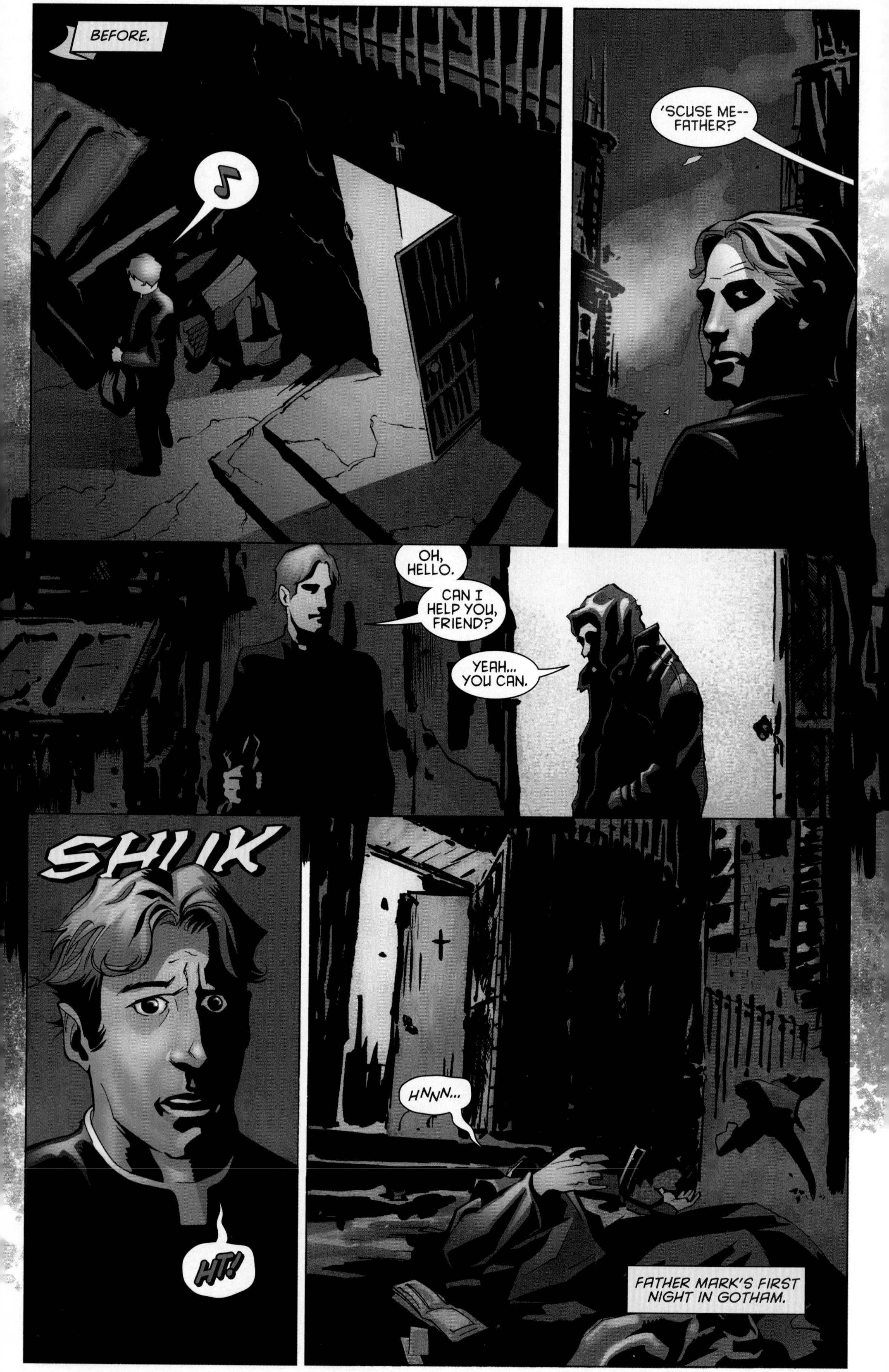
BEFORE.
'SCUSE ME--
FATHER?
OH,
HELLO.
CAN I
HELP YOU,
FRIEND?
YEAH...
YOU CAN.
SHUK
HT!
HNNN...
FATHER MARK'S FIRST
NIGHT IN GOTHAM.

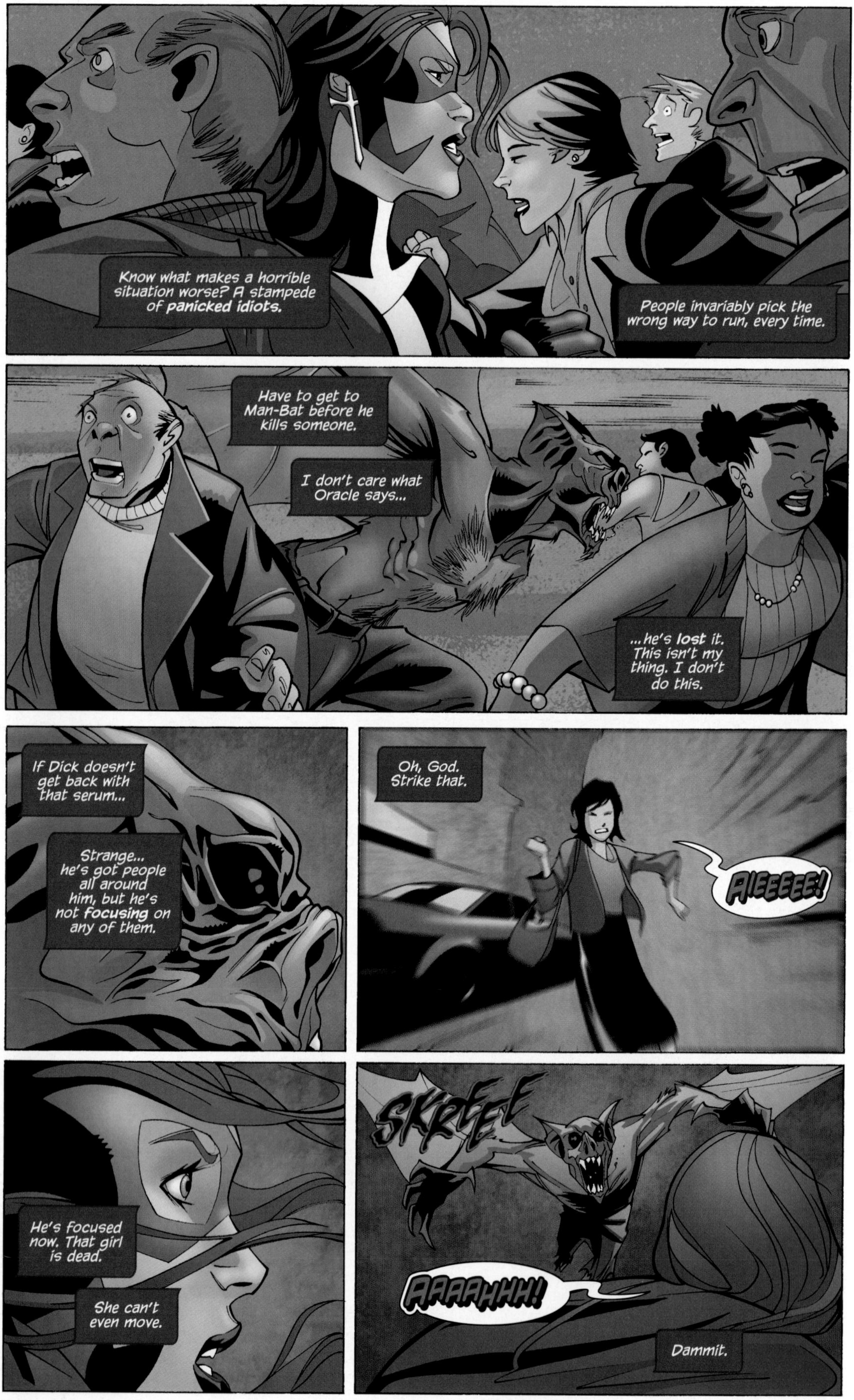

Know what makes a horrible situation worse? A stampede of **panicked idiots.**
People invariably pick the wrong way to run, every time.
Have to get to Man-Bat before he kills someone.
I don't care what Oracle says...
...he's **lost** it. This isn't my thing. I don't do this.
If Dick doesn't get back with that serum...
Strange... he's got people all around him, but he's not **focusing** on any of them.
Oh, God. Strike that.
AIEEEEE!
He's focused now. That girl is dead.
She can't even move.
SKREEE
AAAAHHH!
Dammit.

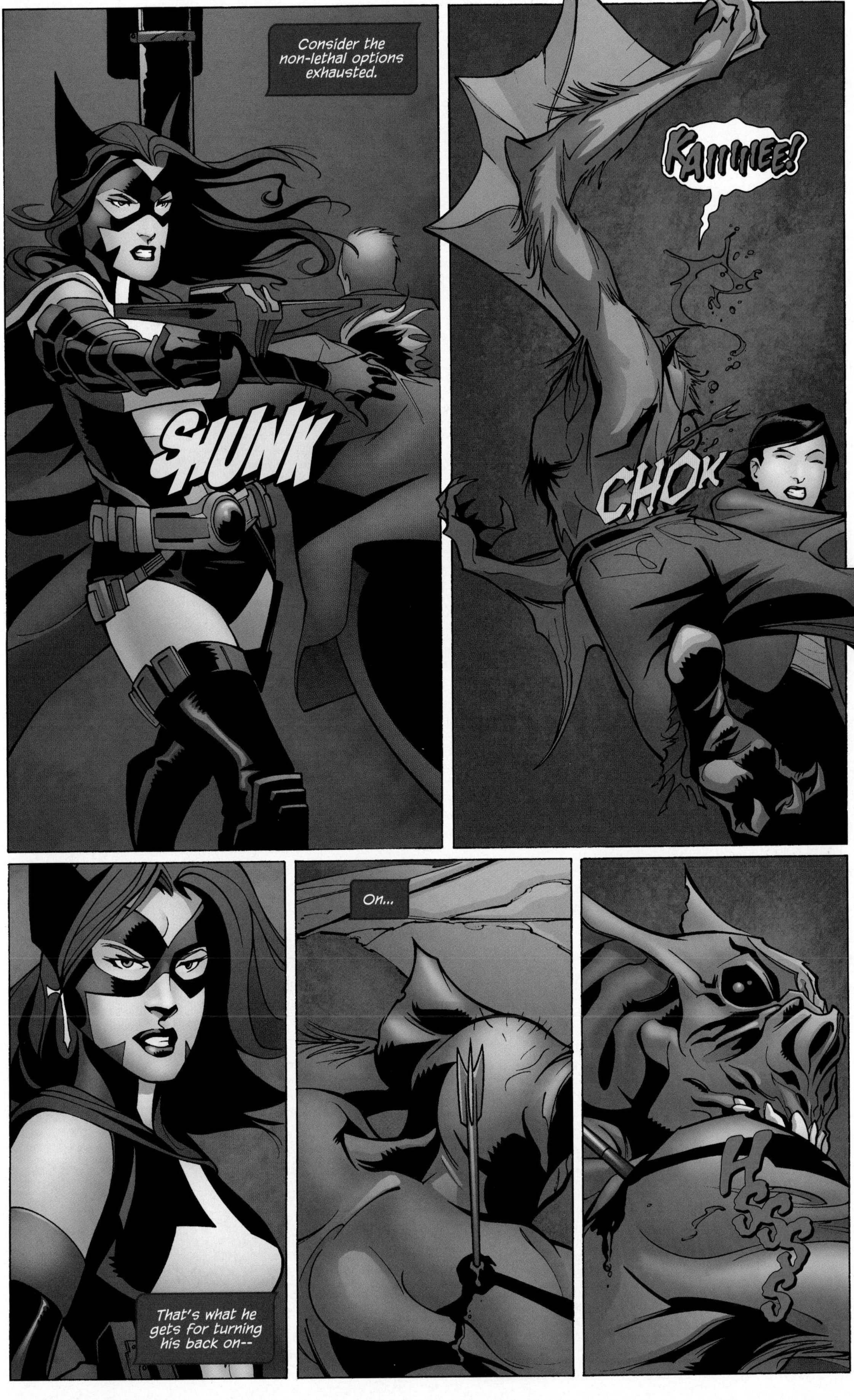
Consider the non-lethal options exhausted.
SHUNK
KAIIIIIEE!
CHOK
That's what he gets for turning his back on--
On...
HSSSSS

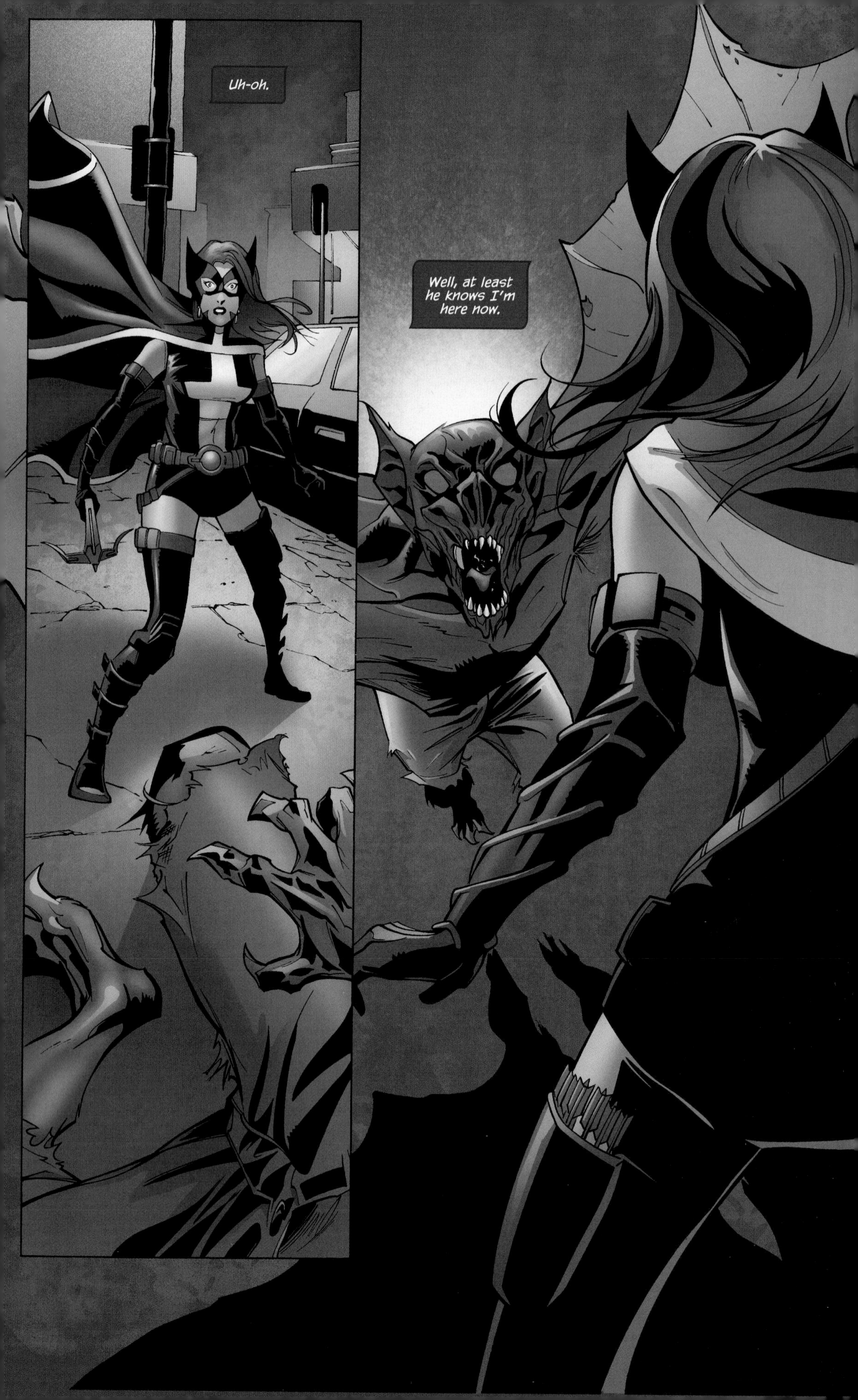
Uh-oh.
Well, at least he knows I'm here now.

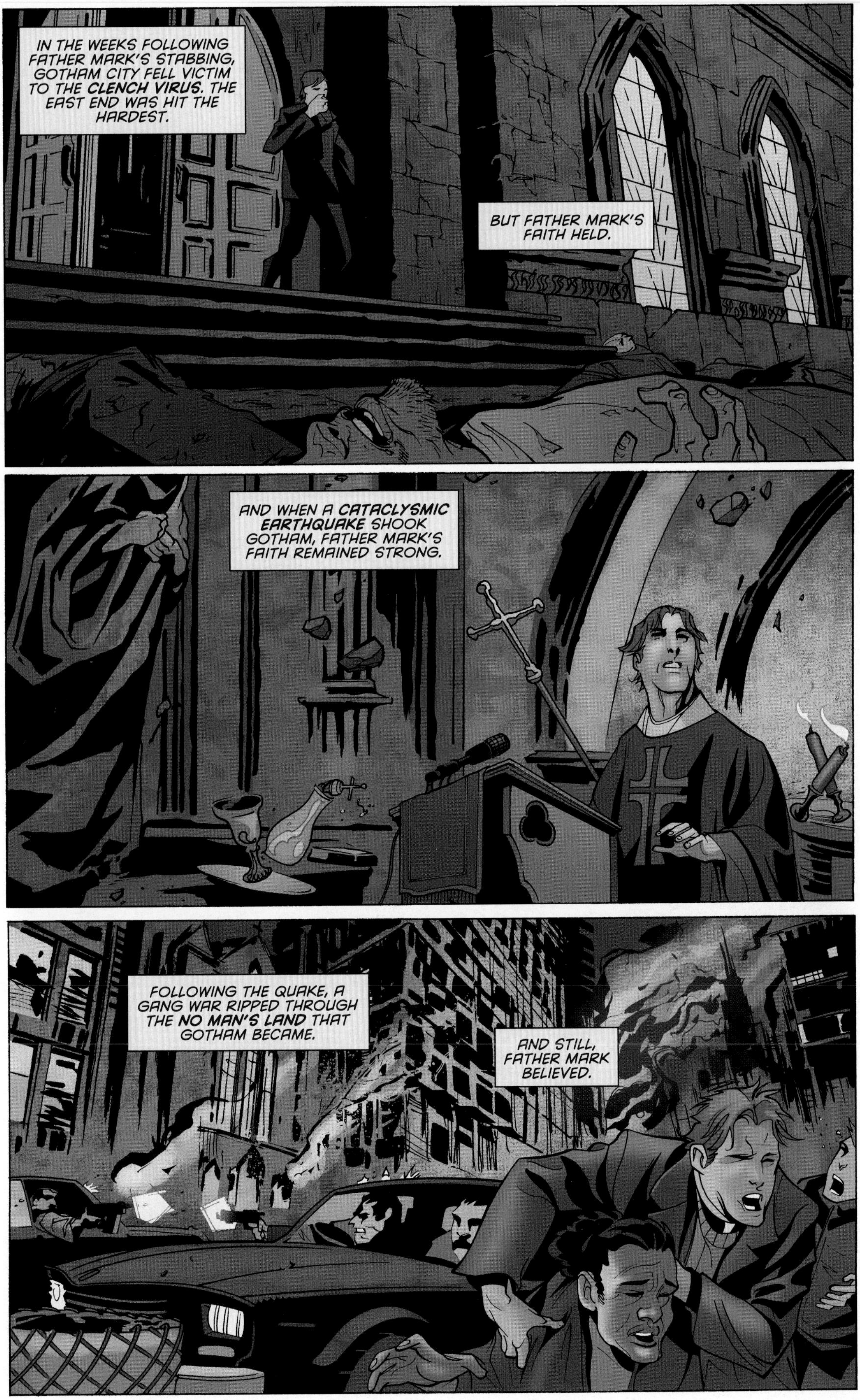
IN THE WEEKS FOLLOWING FATHER MARK'S STABBING, GOTHAM CITY FELL VICTIM TO THE **CLENCH VIRUS**. THE EAST END WAS HIT THE HARDEST.
BUT FATHER MARK'S FAITH HELD.
AND WHEN A **CATACLYSMIC EARTHQUAKE** SHOOK GOTHAM, FATHER MARK'S FAITH REMAINED STRONG.
FOLLOWING THE QUAKE, A GANG WAR RIPPED THROUGH THE **NO MAN'S LAND** THAT GOTHAM BECAME.
AND STILL, FATHER MARK BELIEVED.

THE FIRST VISIBLE CRACKS IN FATHER MARK'S FAITH STARTED TO APPEAR WHEN *EVIL GODS* FROM ANOTHER DIMENSION INVADED THE PLANET.

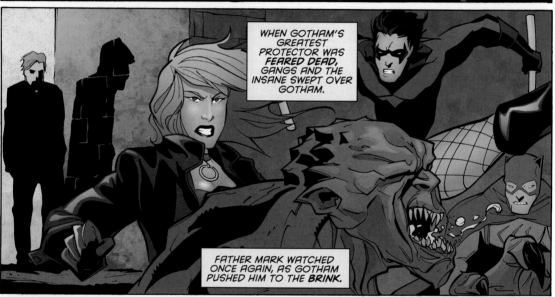

WHEN GOTHAM'S GREATEST PROTECTOR WAS *FEARED DEAD*, GANGS AND THE INSANE SWEPT OVER GOTHAM.

FATHER MARK WATCHED ONCE AGAIN, AS GOTHAM PUSHED HIM TO THE *BRINK.*

HE WATCHED AS THE LEVIATHAN TRIED TO *BURN* HIS FAITH DOWN AROUND HIM.

This is going to *hurt.*

I have to believe that if Kirk Langstrom was any kind of man...

Got it!

If he was any kind of man, he'd want to be put out of his misery.

THAP

He'd see the monster he'd become, and he'd **want** someone to put him down. Before he killed someone.

Like me, for instance. God, he's fast. This is going to be close.

The others don't see it.

They wait for a cure. They hope for rehabilitation. They pretend the system works.

But they all know it doesn't. They know there is **no cure.**

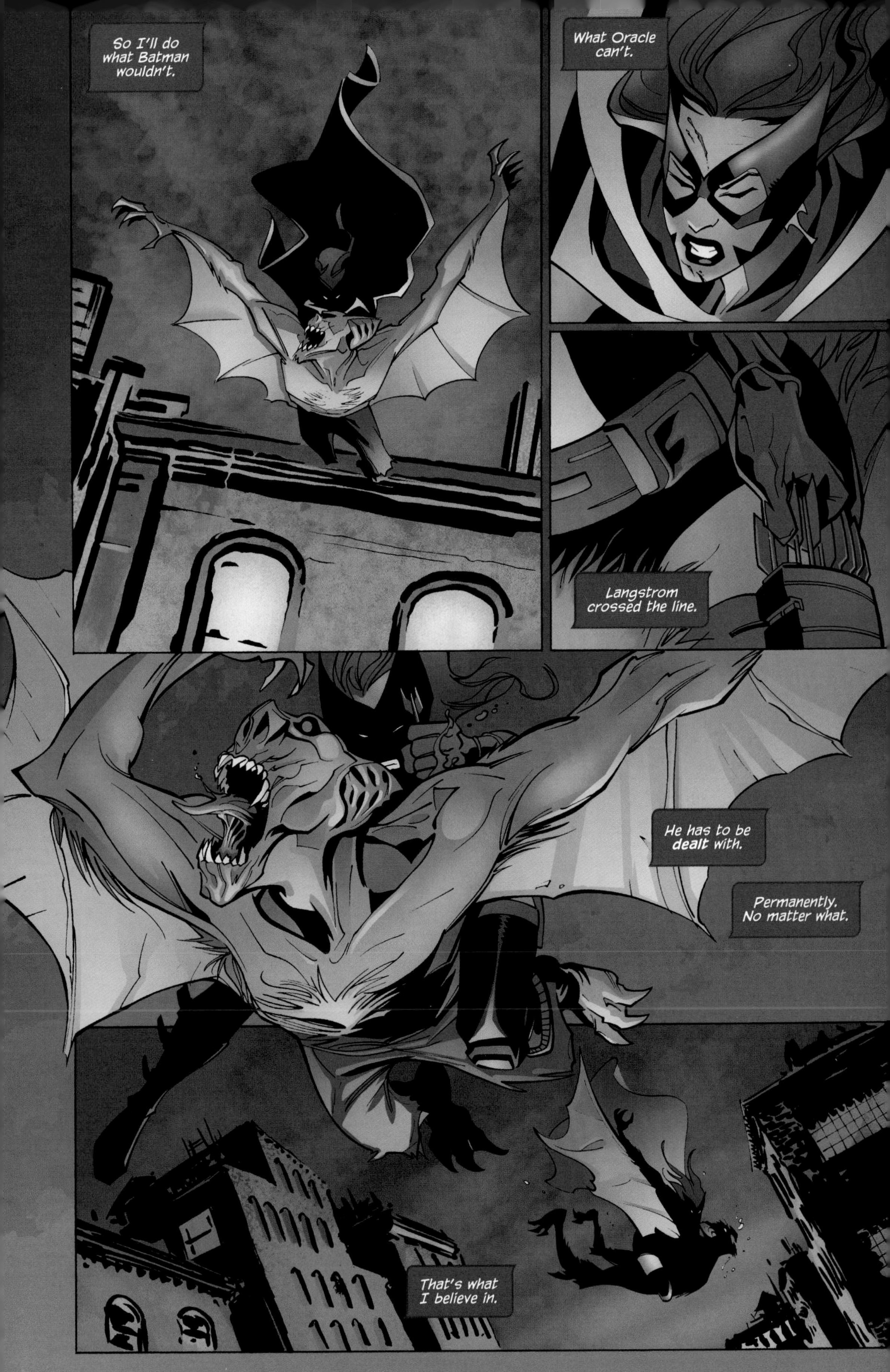
So I'll do what Batman wouldn't.
What Oracle can't.
Langstrom crossed the line.
He has to be **dealt** with.
Permanently. No matter what.
That's what I believe in.

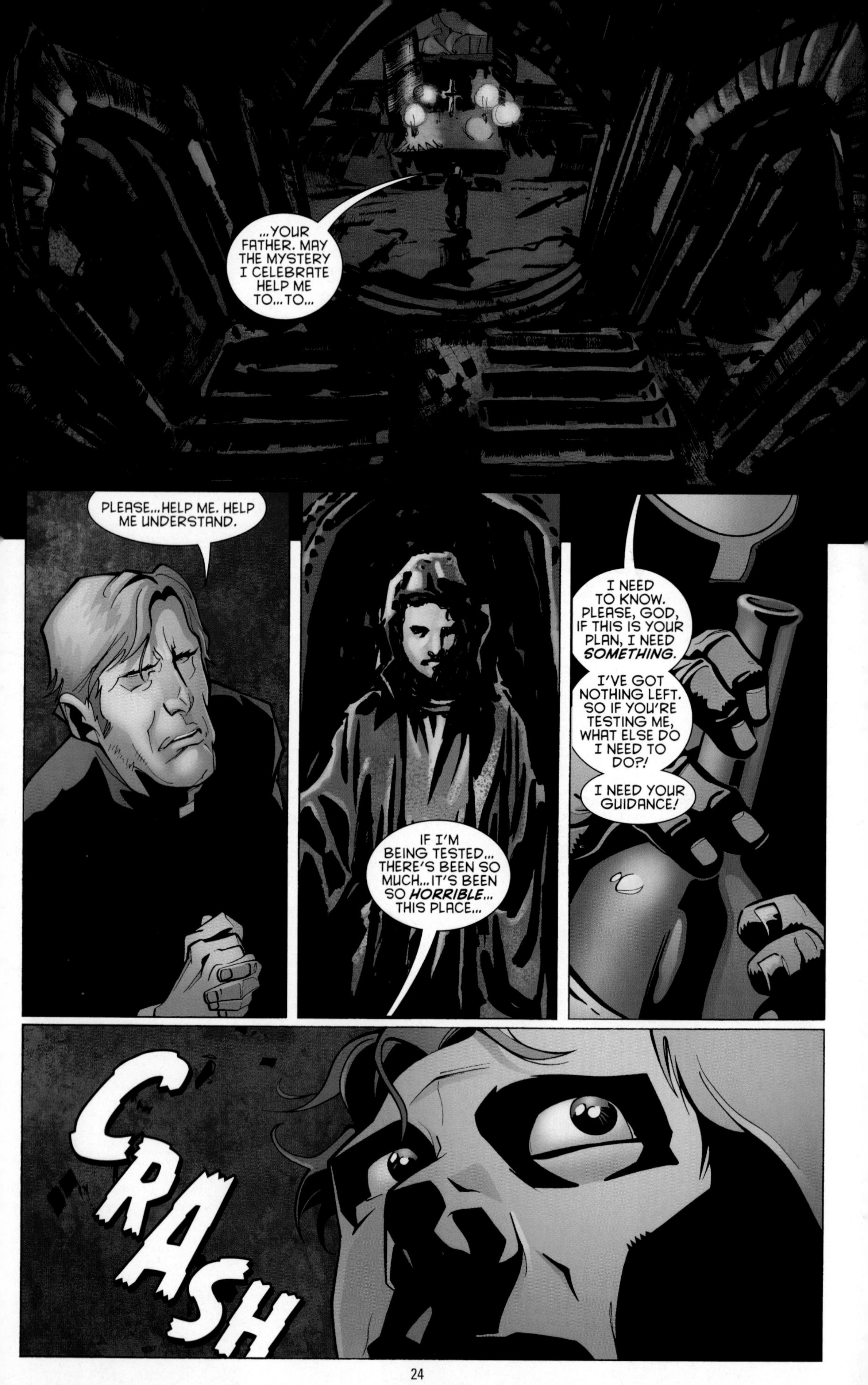
...YOUR FATHER. MAY THE MYSTERY I CELEBRATE HELP ME TO...TO...
PLEASE...HELP ME. HELP ME UNDERSTAND.
IF I'M BEING TESTED... THERE'S BEEN SO MUCH...IT'S BEEN SO *HORRIBLE*... THIS PLACE...
I NEED TO KNOW. PLEASE, GOD, IF THIS IS YOUR PLAN, I NEED *SOMETHING*.
I'VE GOT NOTHING LEFT. SO IF YOU'RE TESTING ME, WHAT ELSE DO I NEED TO DO?!
I NEED YOUR GUIDANCE!
CRASH

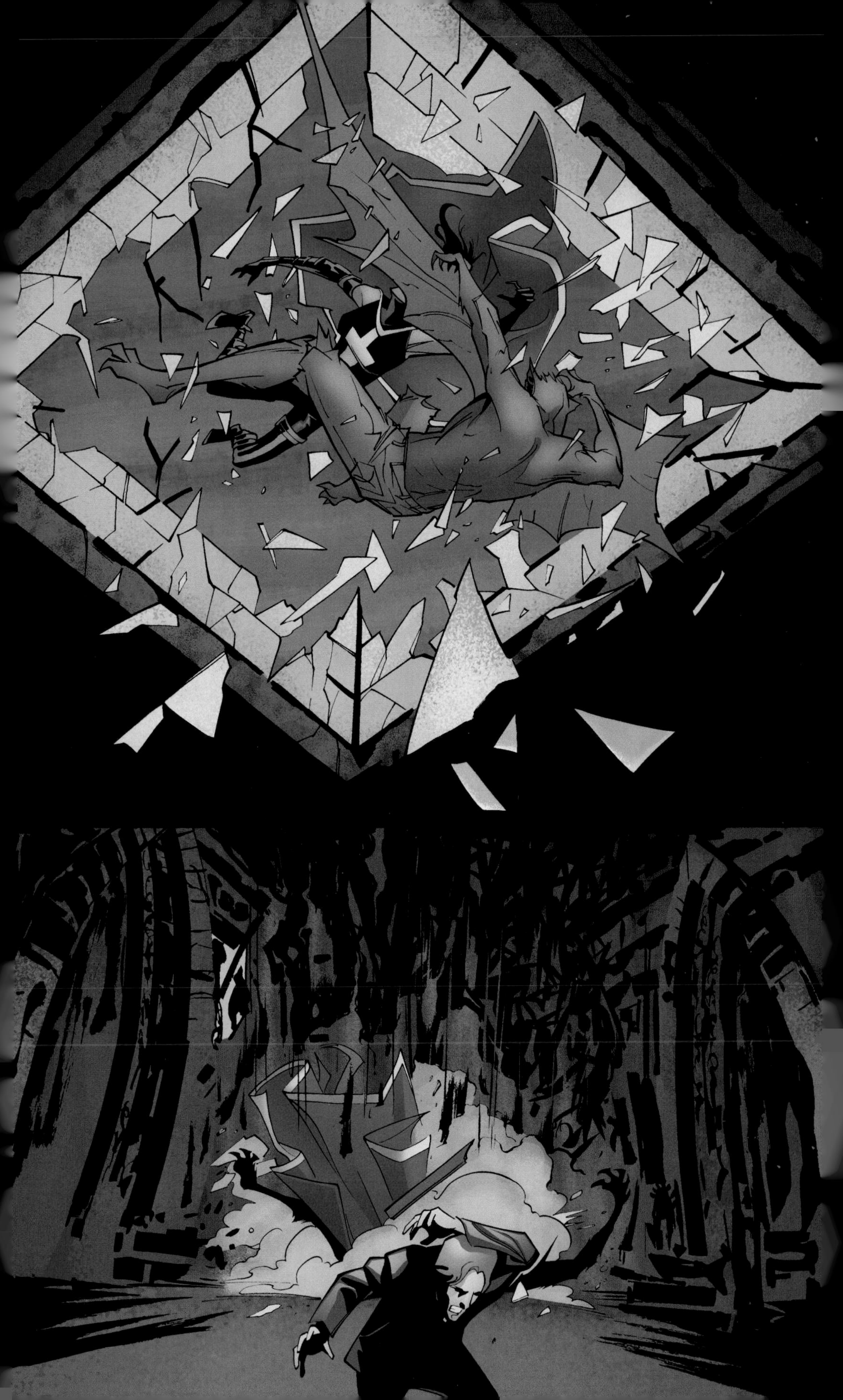

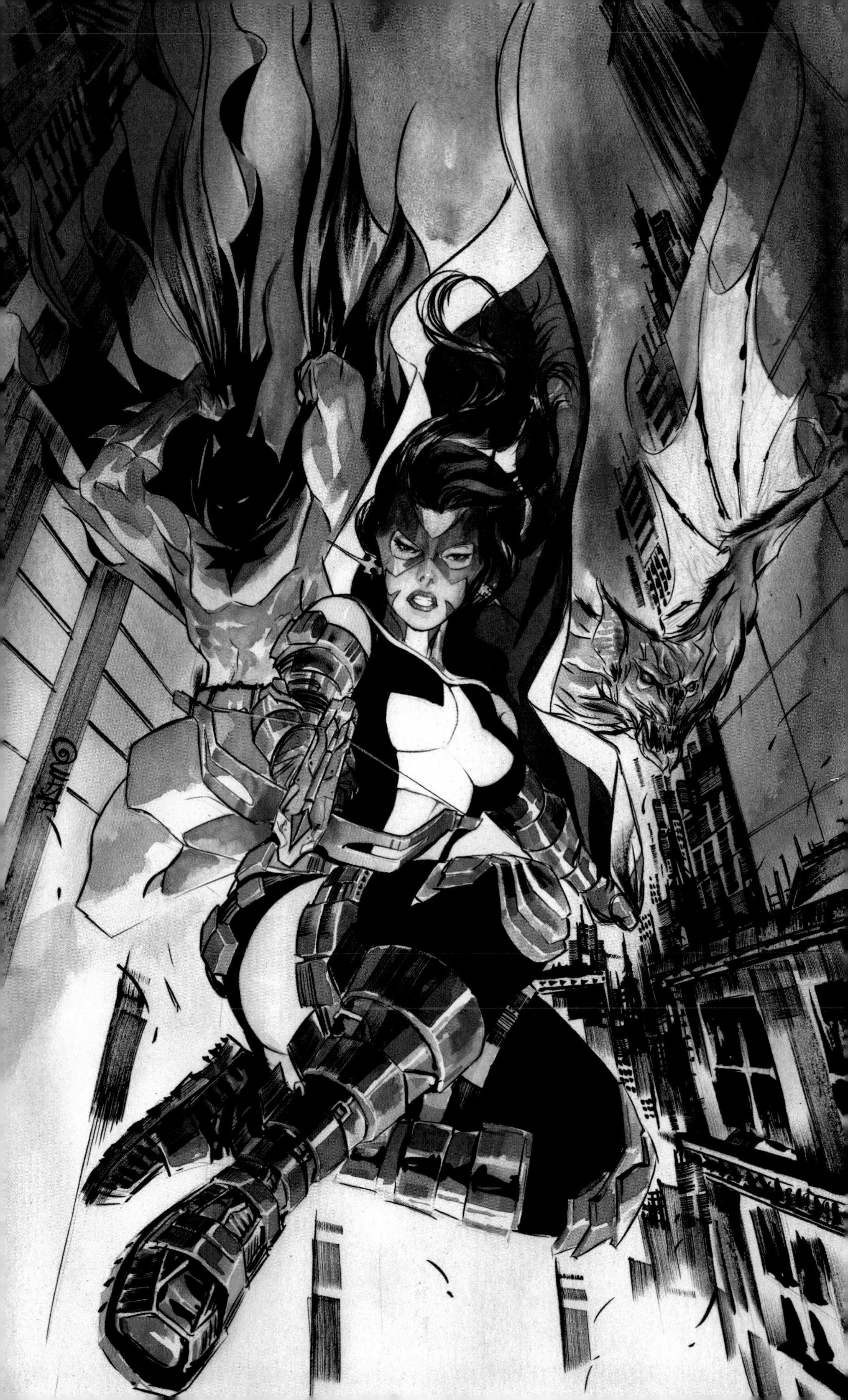

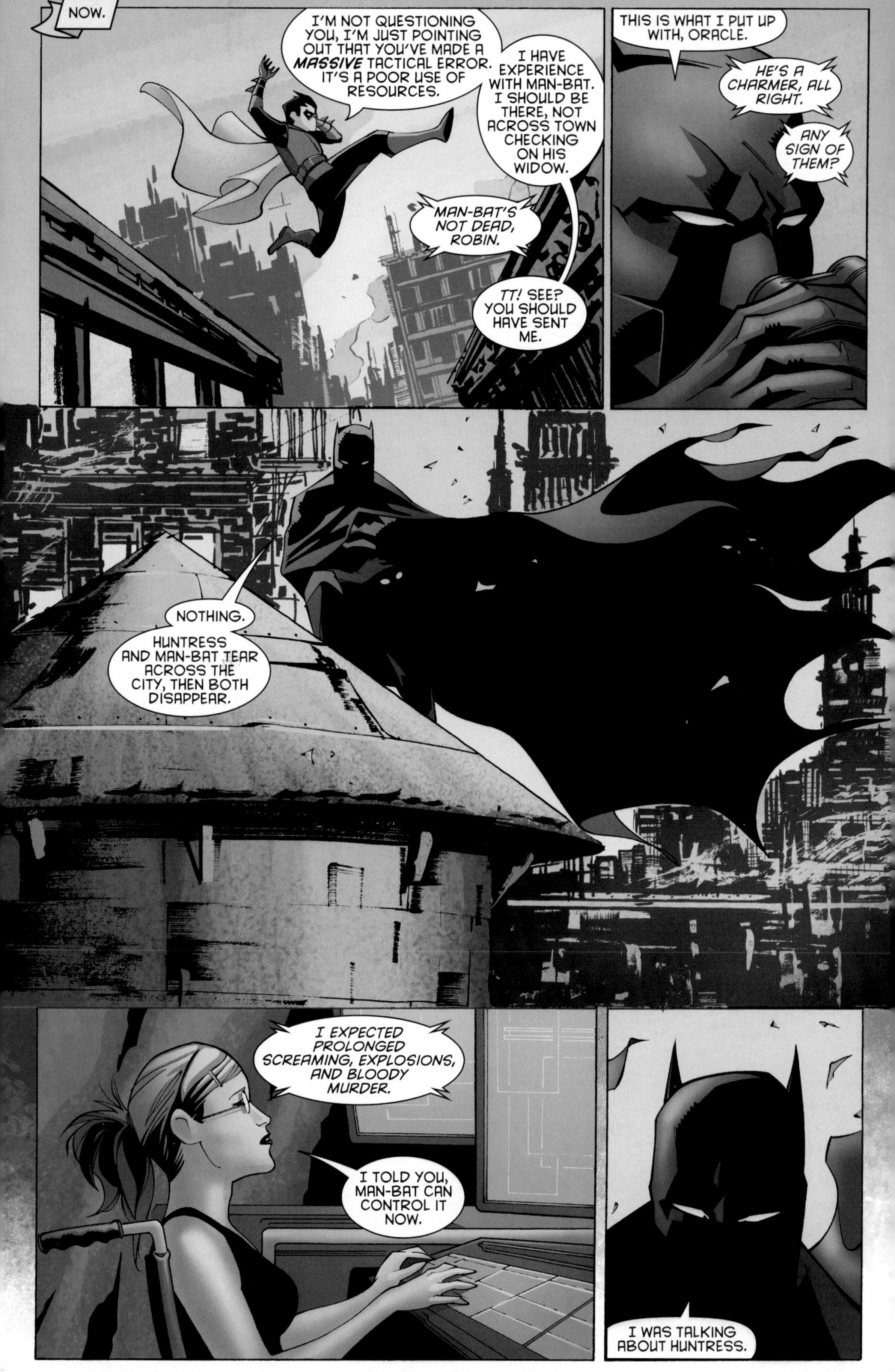
NOW.
I'M NOT QUESTIONING YOU, I'M JUST POINTING OUT THAT YOU'VE MADE A MASSIVE TACTICAL ERROR. IT'S A POOR USE OF RESOURCES.
I HAVE EXPERIENCE WITH MAN-BAT. I SHOULD BE THERE, NOT ACROSS TOWN CHECKING ON HIS WIDOW.
MAN-BAT'S NOT DEAD, ROBIN.
TT! SEE? YOU SHOULD HAVE SENT ME.
THIS IS WHAT I PUT UP WITH, ORACLE.
HE'S A CHARMER, ALL RIGHT.
ANY SIGN OF THEM?
NOTHING.
HUNTRESS AND MAN-BAT TEAR ACROSS THE CITY, THEN BOTH DISAPPEAR.
I EXPECTED PROLONGED SCREAMING, EXPLOSIONS, AND BLOODY MURDER.
I TOLD YOU, MAN-BAT CAN CONTROL IT NOW.
I WAS TALKING ABOUT HUNTRESS.

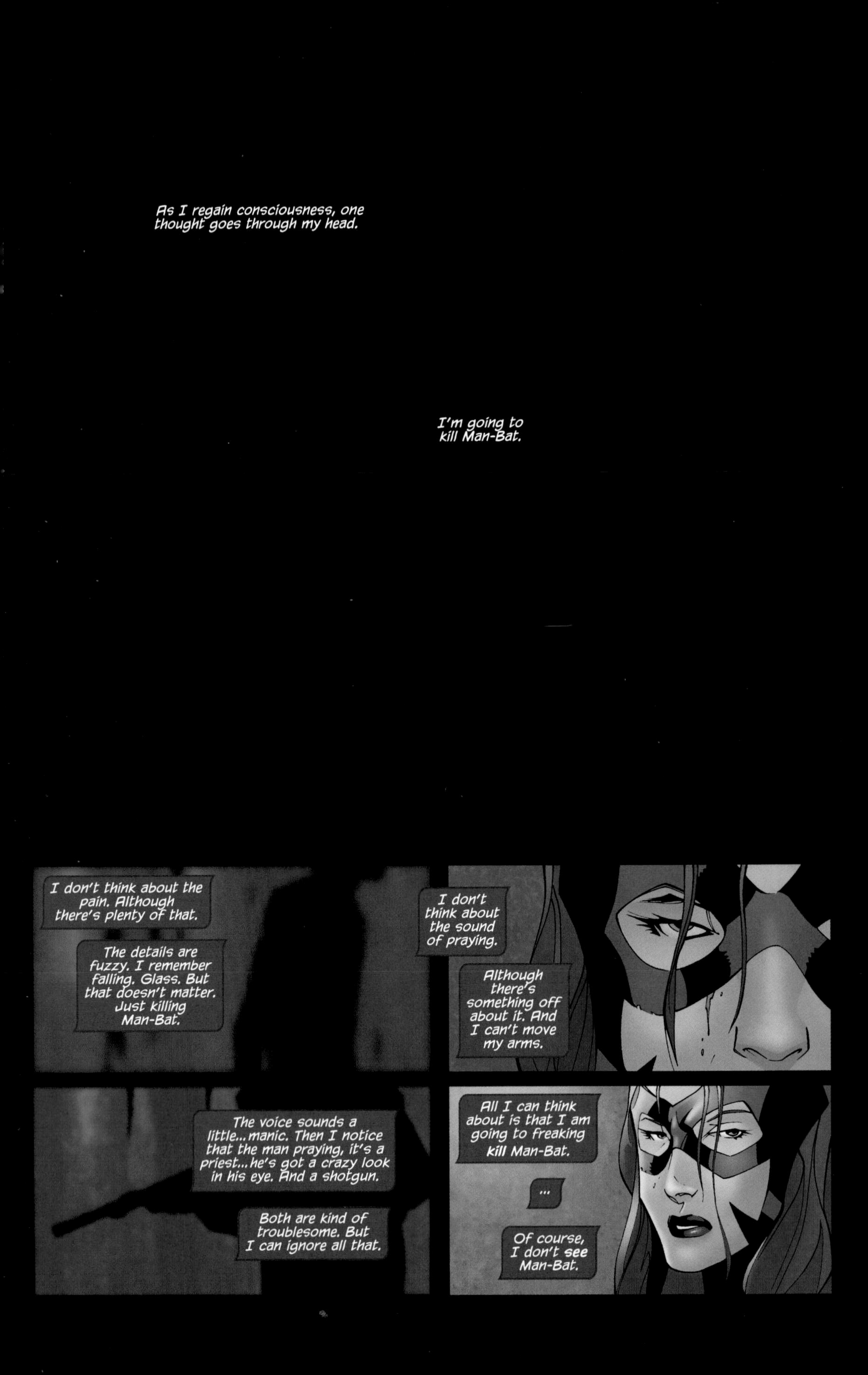
As I regain consciousness, one thought goes through my head.
I'm going to kill Man-Bat.
I don't think about the pain. Although there's plenty of that.
The details are fuzzy. I remember falling. Glass. But that doesn't matter. Just killing Man-Bat.
I don't think about the sound of praying.
Although there's something off about it. And I can't move my arms.
The voice sounds a little...manic. Then I notice that the man praying, it's a priest...he's got a crazy look in his eye. And a shotgun.
Both are kind of troublesome. But I can ignore all that.
All I can think about is that I am going to freaking kill Man-Bat.
...
Of course, I don't see Man-Bat.

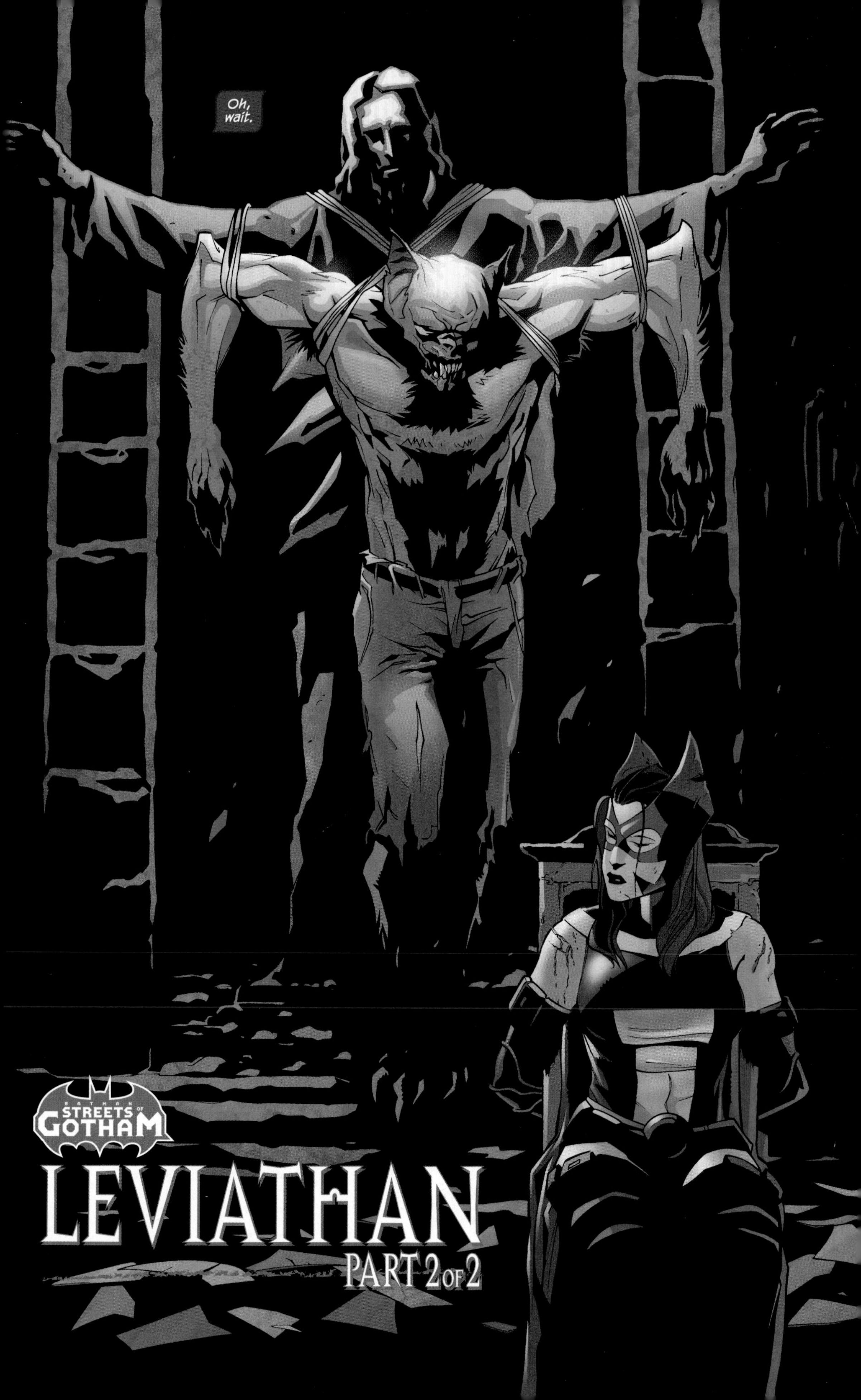
Oh, wait.
BATMAN STREETS OF GOTHAM
LEVIATHAN
PART 2 OF 2

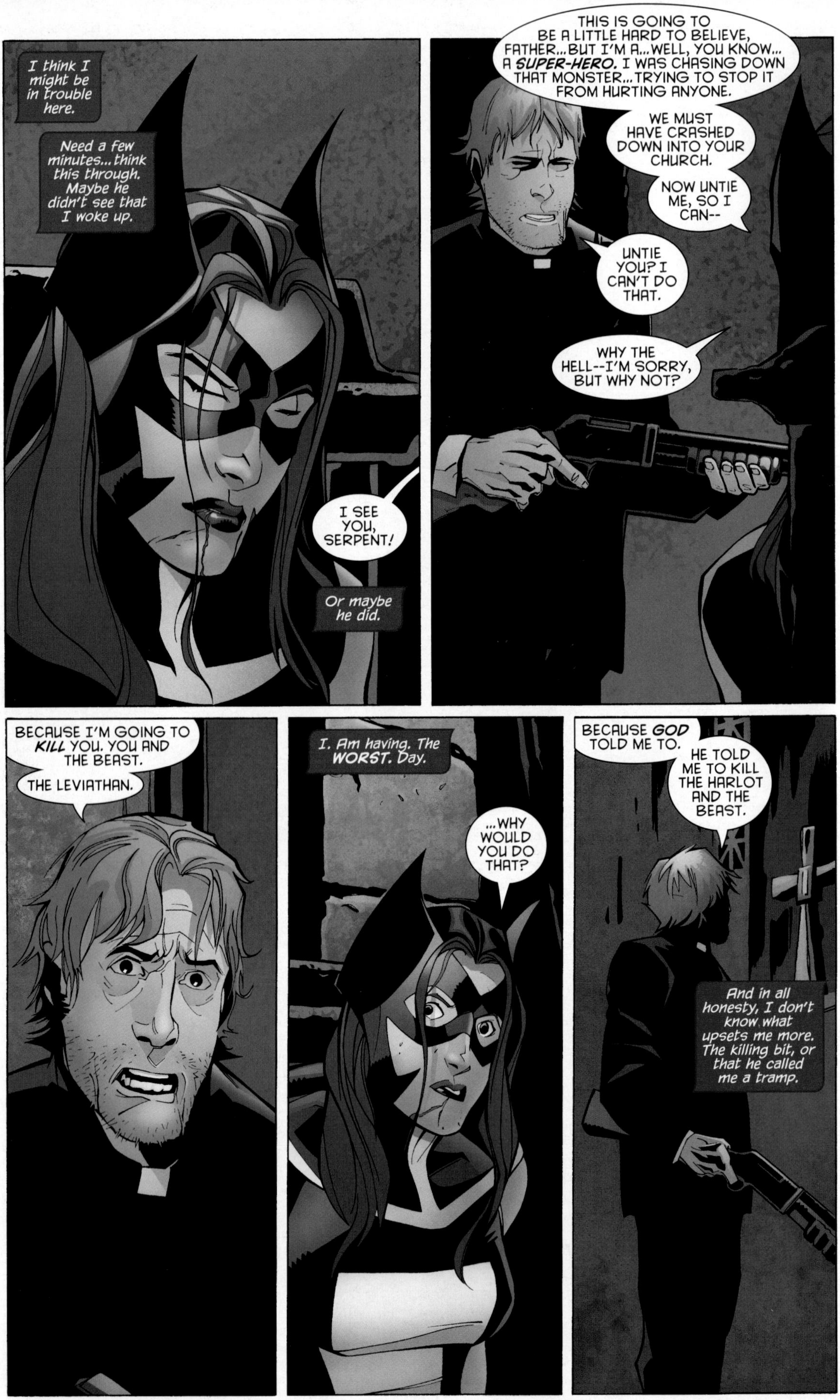

I think I might be in trouble here.
Need a few minutes... think this through. Maybe he didn't see that I woke up.
I SEE YOU, SERPENT!
Or maybe he did.
THIS IS GOING TO BE A LITTLE HARD TO BELIEVE, FATHER... BUT I'M A... WELL, YOU KNOW... A SUPER-HERO. I WAS CHASING DOWN THAT MONSTER... TRYING TO STOP IT FROM HURTING ANYONE.
WE MUST HAVE CRASHED DOWN INTO YOUR CHURCH.
NOW UNTIE ME, SO I CAN--
UNTIE YOU? I CAN'T DO THAT.
WHY THE HELL--I'M SORRY, BUT WHY NOT?
BECAUSE I'M GOING TO KILL YOU. YOU AND THE BEAST.
THE LEVIATHAN.
I. Am having. The WORST. Day.
...WHY WOULD YOU DO THAT?
BECAUSE GOD TOLD ME TO.
HE TOLD ME TO KILL THE HARLOT AND THE BEAST.
And in all honesty, I don't know what upsets me more. The killing bit, or that he called me a tramp.

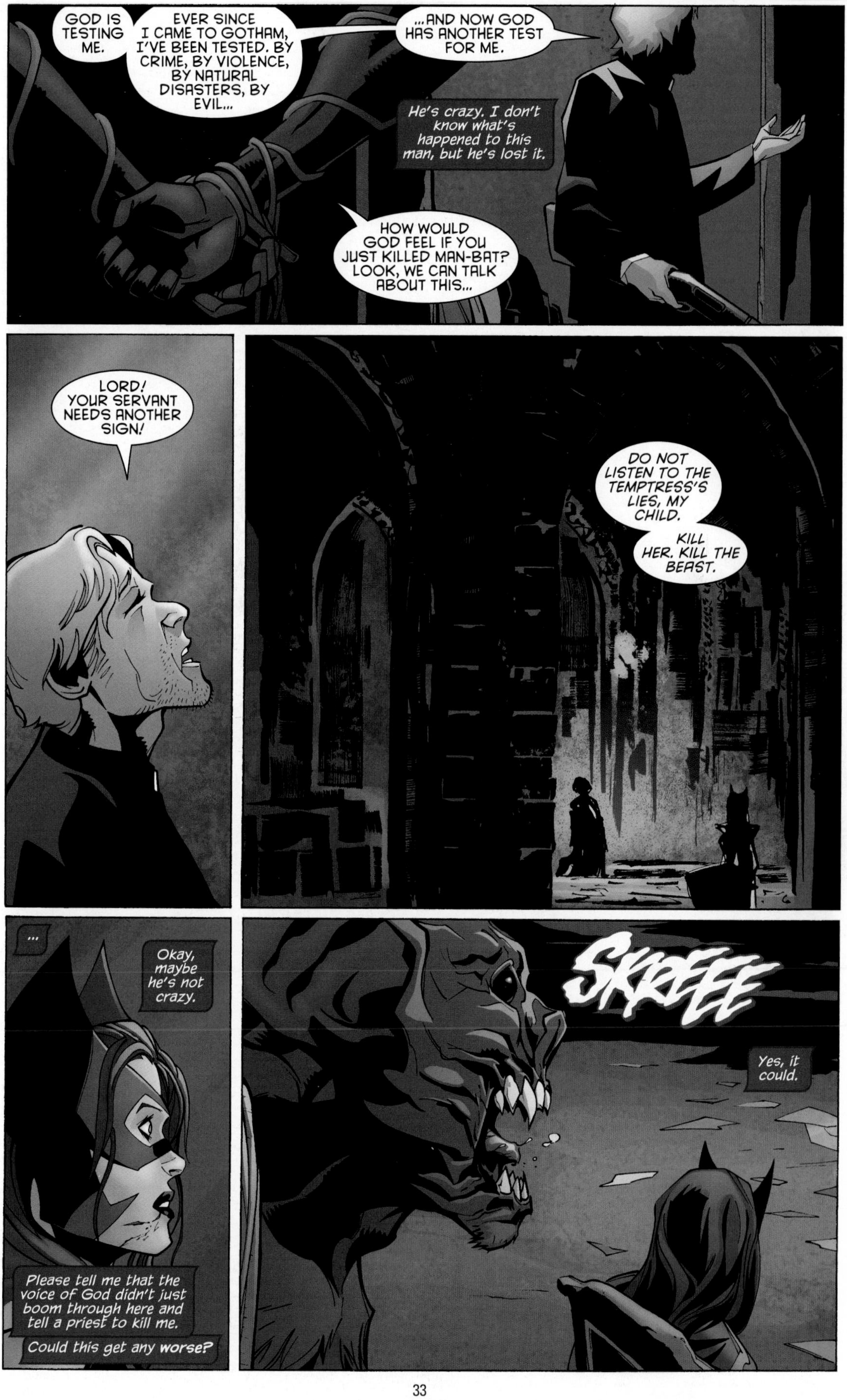
GOD IS TESTING ME.
EVER SINCE I CAME TO GOTHAM, I'VE BEEN TESTED. BY CRIME, BY VIOLENCE, BY NATURAL DISASTERS, BY EVIL...
...AND NOW GOD HAS ANOTHER TEST FOR ME.
He's crazy. I don't know what's happened to this man, but he's lost it.
HOW WOULD GOD FEEL IF YOU JUST KILLED MAN-BAT? LOOK, WE CAN TALK ABOUT THIS...
LORD! YOUR SERVANT NEEDS ANOTHER SIGN!
DO NOT LISTEN TO THE TEMPTRESS'S LIES, MY CHILD.
KILL HER. KILL THE BEAST.
...
Okay, maybe he's not crazy.
Please tell me that the voice of God didn't just boom through here and tell a priest to kill me.
Could this get any **worse?**
SKREEE
Yes, it could.

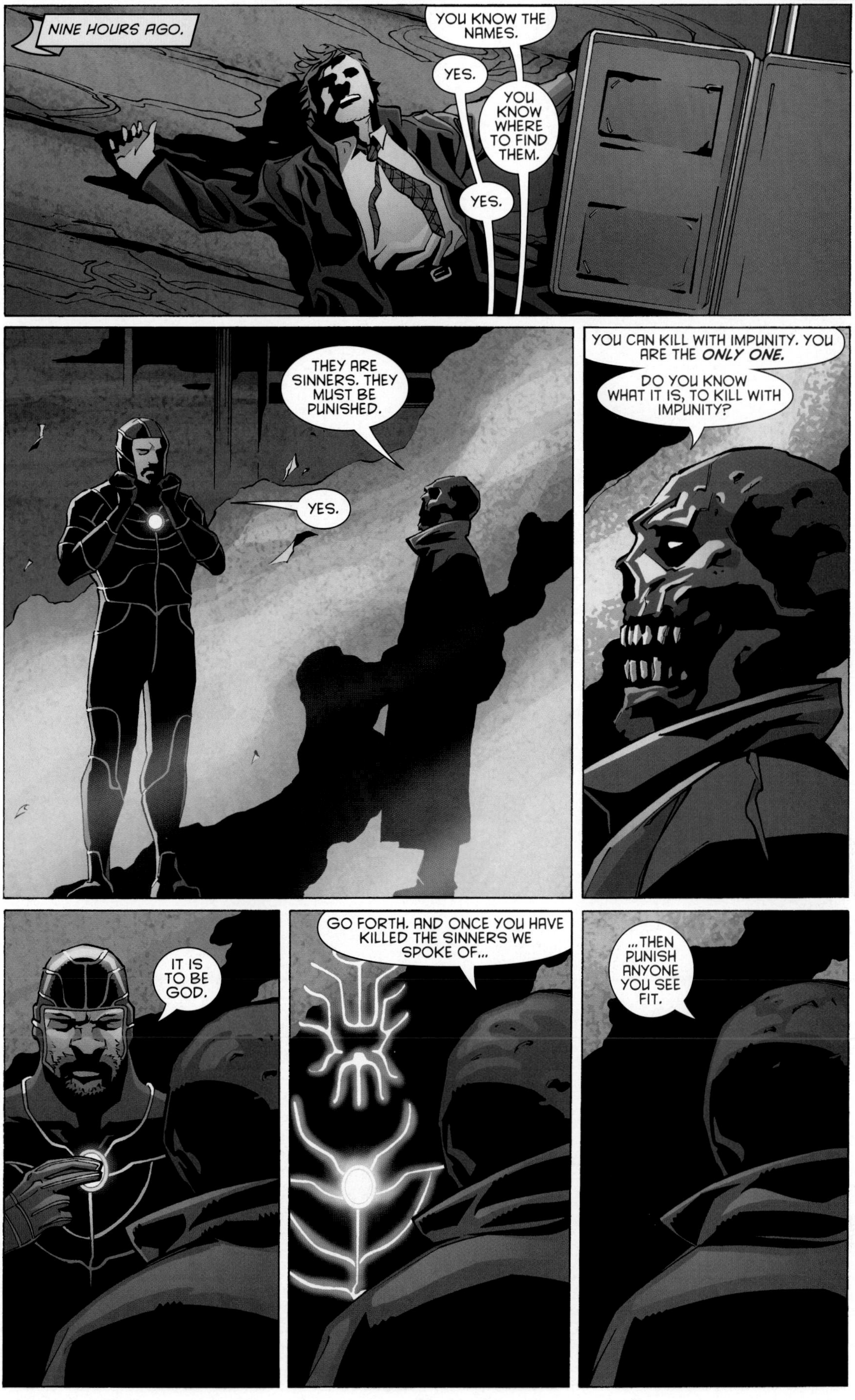
NINE HOURS AGO.
YOU KNOW THE NAMES.
YES.
YOU KNOW WHERE TO FIND THEM.
YES.
THEY ARE SINNERS. THEY MUST BE PUNISHED.
YES.
YOU CAN KILL WITH IMPUNITY. YOU ARE THE *ONLY ONE.*
DO YOU KNOW WHAT IT IS, TO KILL WITH IMPUNITY?
IT IS TO BE GOD.
GO FORTH. AND ONCE YOU HAVE KILLED THE SINNERS WE SPOKE OF...
...THEN PUNISH ANYONE YOU SEE FIT.

SKREEE

Langstrom's lost it.

SKREEE

SKREEE

He's about three seconds away from breaking through those ropes and slaughtering the priest.

Why? Why attack the priest? He's ignored me all day...and I put a crossbow bolt through him.

Why would he care about--

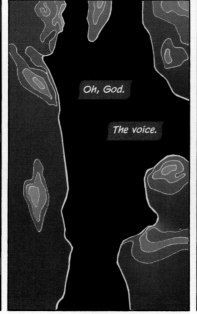

Oh, God.

The voice.

There's someone here.

There's someone else here, and Man-Bat can see him.

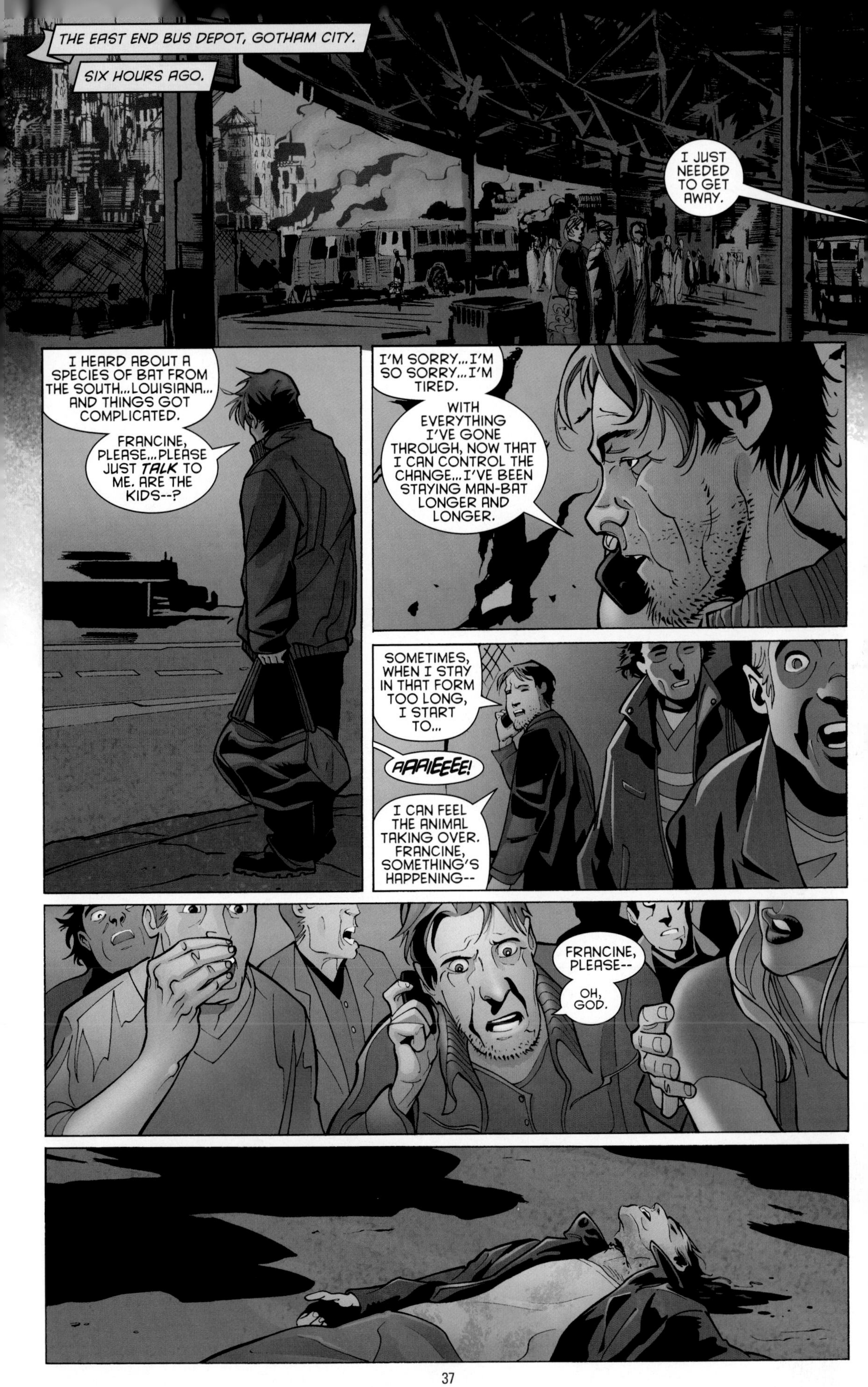

THE EAST END BUS DEPOT, GOTHAM CITY.
SIX HOURS AGO.
I JUST NEEDED TO GET AWAY.
I HEARD ABOUT A SPECIES OF BAT FROM THE SOUTH...LOUISIANA... AND THINGS GOT COMPLICATED.
FRANCINE, PLEASE...PLEASE JUST TALK TO ME. ARE THE KIDS--?
I'M SORRY...I'M SO SORRY...I'M TIRED.
WITH EVERYTHING I'VE GONE THROUGH, NOW THAT I CAN CONTROL THE CHANGE...I'VE BEEN STAYING MAN-BAT LONGER AND LONGER.
SOMETIMES, WHEN I STAY IN THAT FORM TOO LONG, I START TO...
AAAIEEEE!
I CAN FEEL THE ANIMAL TAKING OVER. FRANCINE, SOMETHING'S HAPPENING--
FRANCINE, PLEASE--
OH, GOD.

I DON'T...

SHLIKK

ARRGHH!

AAAHHH--*

NO...
THAT'S NOT
POSSIBLE...

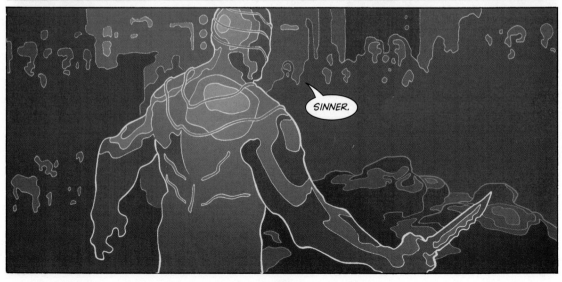

SINNER.

LORD! PROTECT ME! GIVE ME YOUR STRENGTH!

I was going to do it. I was going to kill Man-Bat.

He was hunting something... and I was going to kill him.

LET ME HEAR YOUR *VOICE!* GIVE YOUR SERVANT *HOPE!*

LISTEN TO ME!

THAT'S NOT THE VOICE OF GOD, FATHER! YOU HAVE TO RUN! GET OUT OF HERE!

BE SILENT! I AM TRYING TO COMMUNE WITH THE LORD!

God help me, had I actually managed to do it...

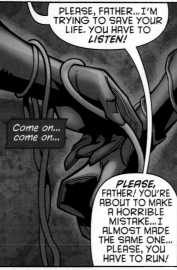

PLEASE, FATHER...I'M TRYING TO SAVE YOUR LIFE. YOU HAVE TO *LISTEN!*

Come on... come on...

PLEASE, FATHER! YOU'RE ABOUT TO MAKE A HORRIBLE MISTAKE...I ALMOST MADE THE SAME ONE... PLEASE, YOU HAVE TO RUN!

HEED THE WORD OF THE LORD, MY CHILD.

THE WOMAN SPEAKS LIES. I AM THE TRUTH. AND I DEMAND THE BEAST'S BLOOD.

YES, MY LORD...

SNAP SNAP

SNAP

Out of time.

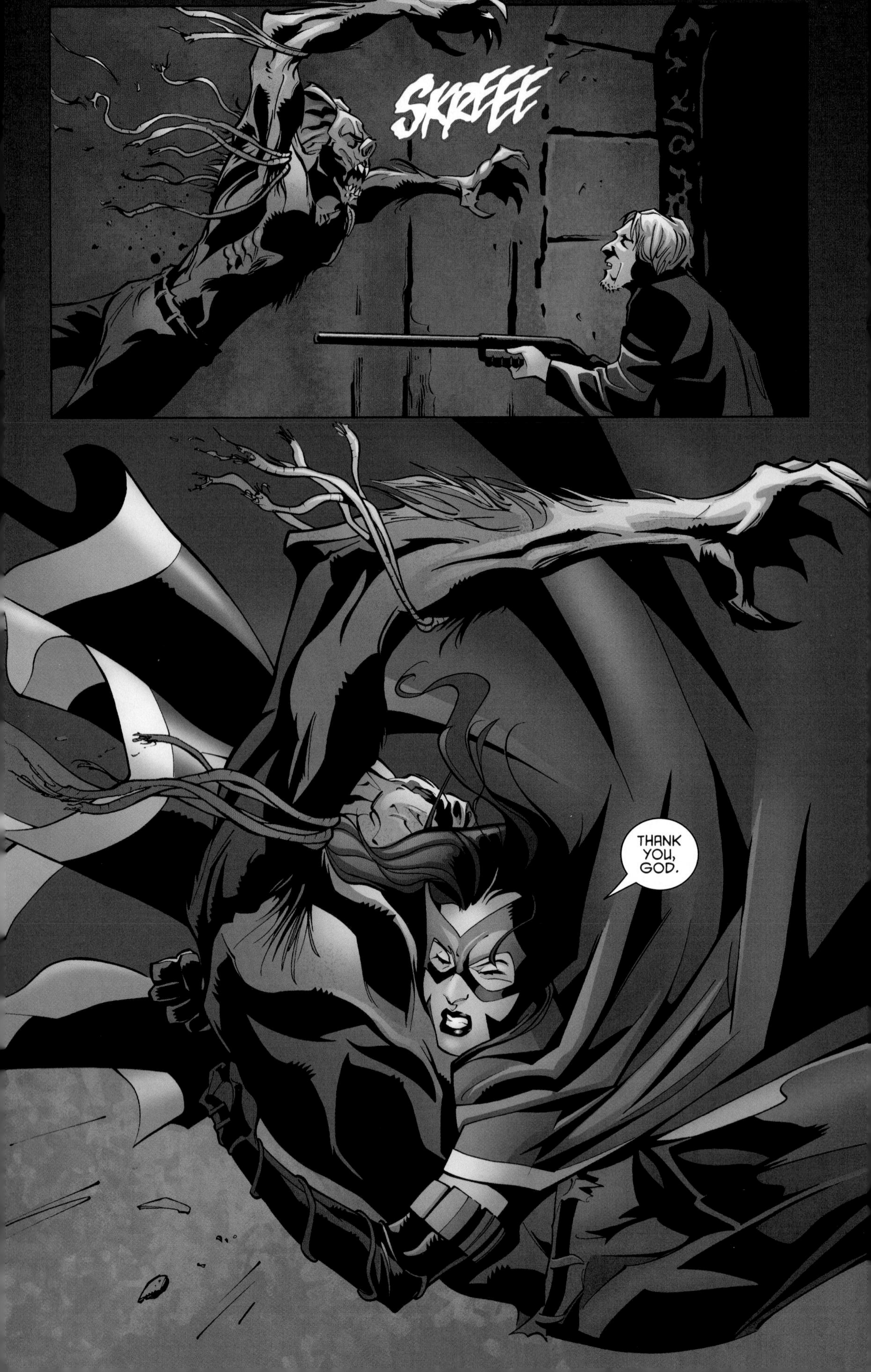
SKREEE
THANK YOU, GOD.

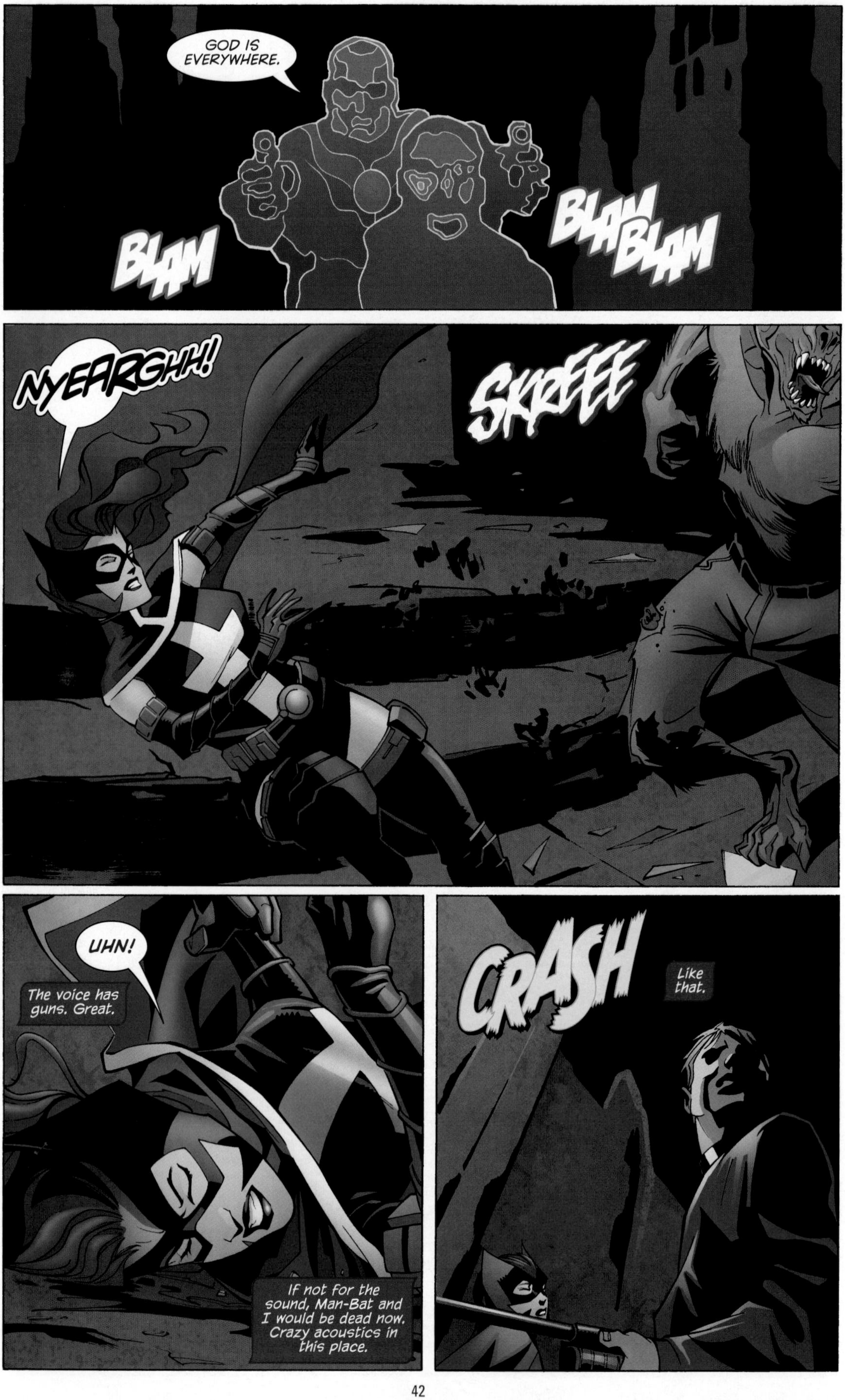
GOD IS EVERYWHERE.
BLAM
BLAM BLAM
NYEARGHH!
SKREEE
UHN!
The voice has guns. Great.
If not for the sound, Man-Bat and I would be dead now. Crazy acoustics in this place.
CRASH
Like that.

43

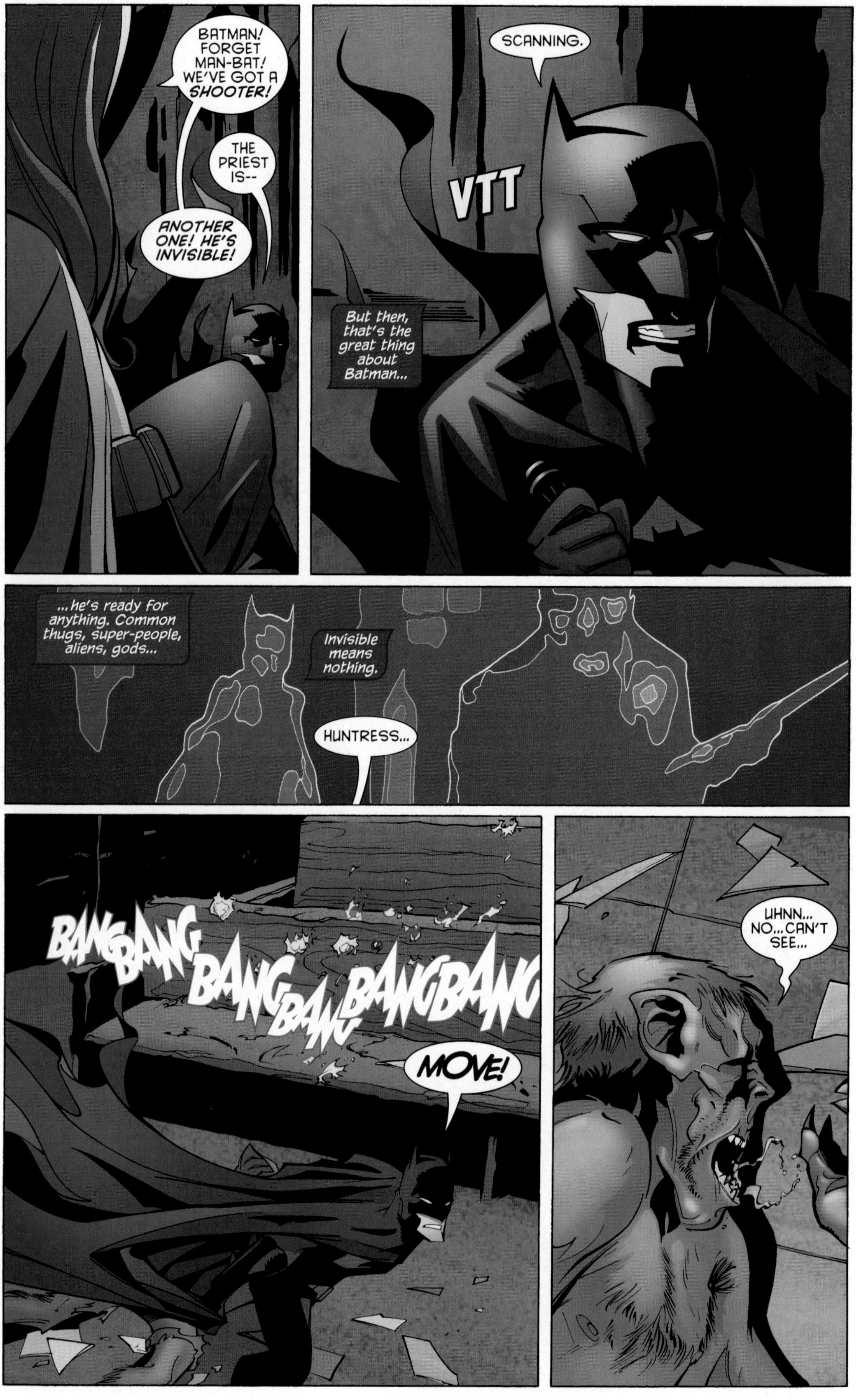
BATMAN! FORGET MAN-BAT! WE'VE GOT A SHOOTER!
THE PRIEST IS--
ANOTHER ONE! HE'S INVISIBLE!
SCANNING.
VTT
But then, that's the great thing about Batman...
...he's ready for anything. Common thugs, super-people, aliens, gods...
Invisible means nothing.
HUNTRESS...
BANGBANG BANGBANG BANGBANG
MOVE!
UHNN... NO...CAN'T SEE...

DID YOU SEE HIM?

NOT BEFORE HE STARTED SHOOTING. STILL CAN'T PINPOINT HIM...THE ACOUSTICS IN HERE AREN'T HELPING.

I WAS GLAD TO SEE LANGSTROM STILL ALIVE.

I...I ALMOST--

KA-CHAK

I FORGOT TO TELL YOU ABOUT THE PRIEST.

WHAT OF THIS ONE, LORD?

DO YOU WANT *HIM* DEAD, TOO?

VTT

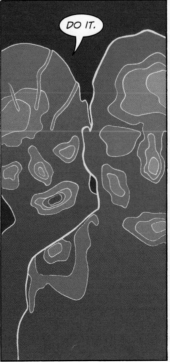

DO IT.

KILL THEM ALL.

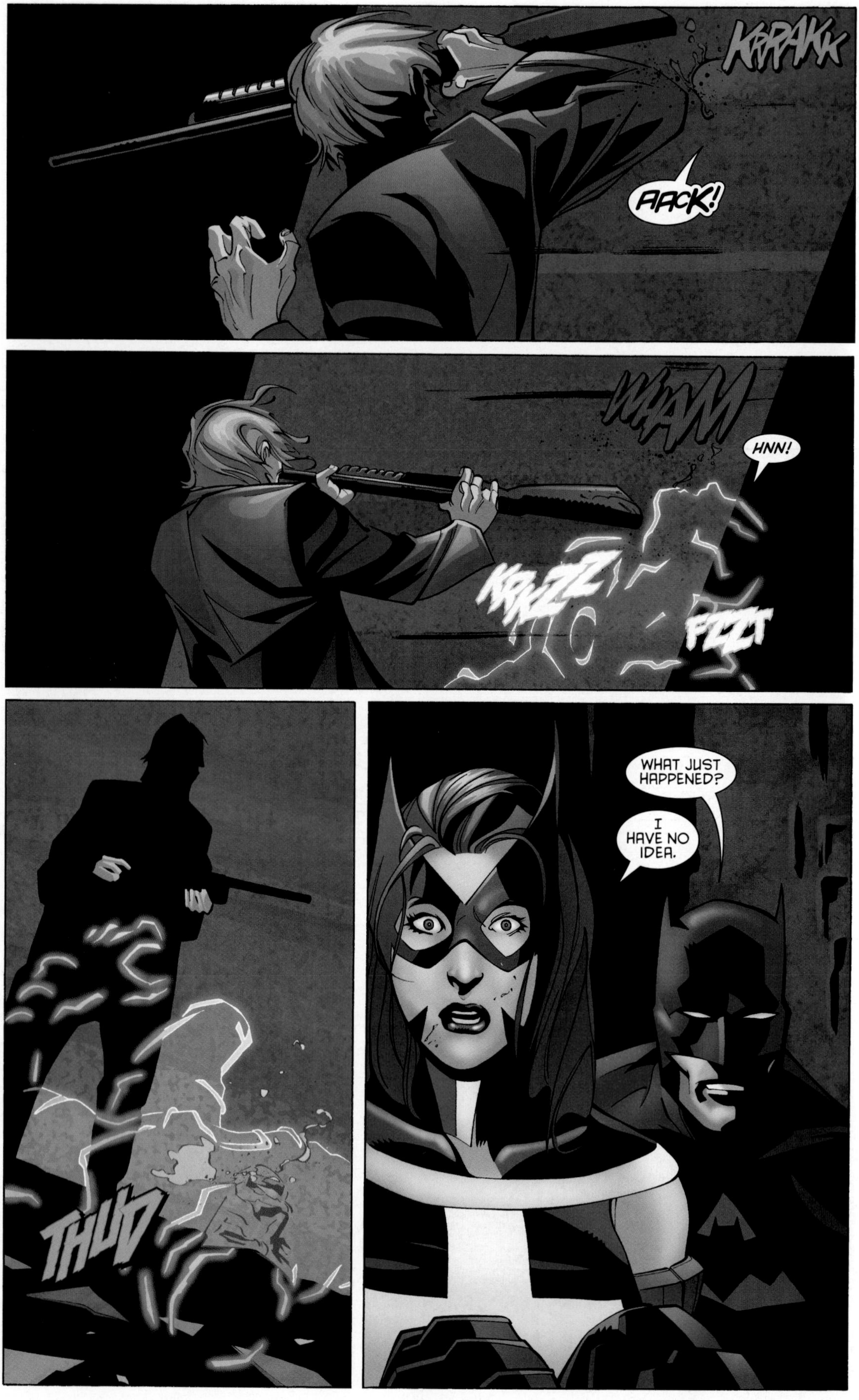
KRRAKK
AACK!
WHAM
HNN!
KRKZZZ
FZZZT
THUD
WHAT JUST HAPPENED?
I HAVE NO IDEA.

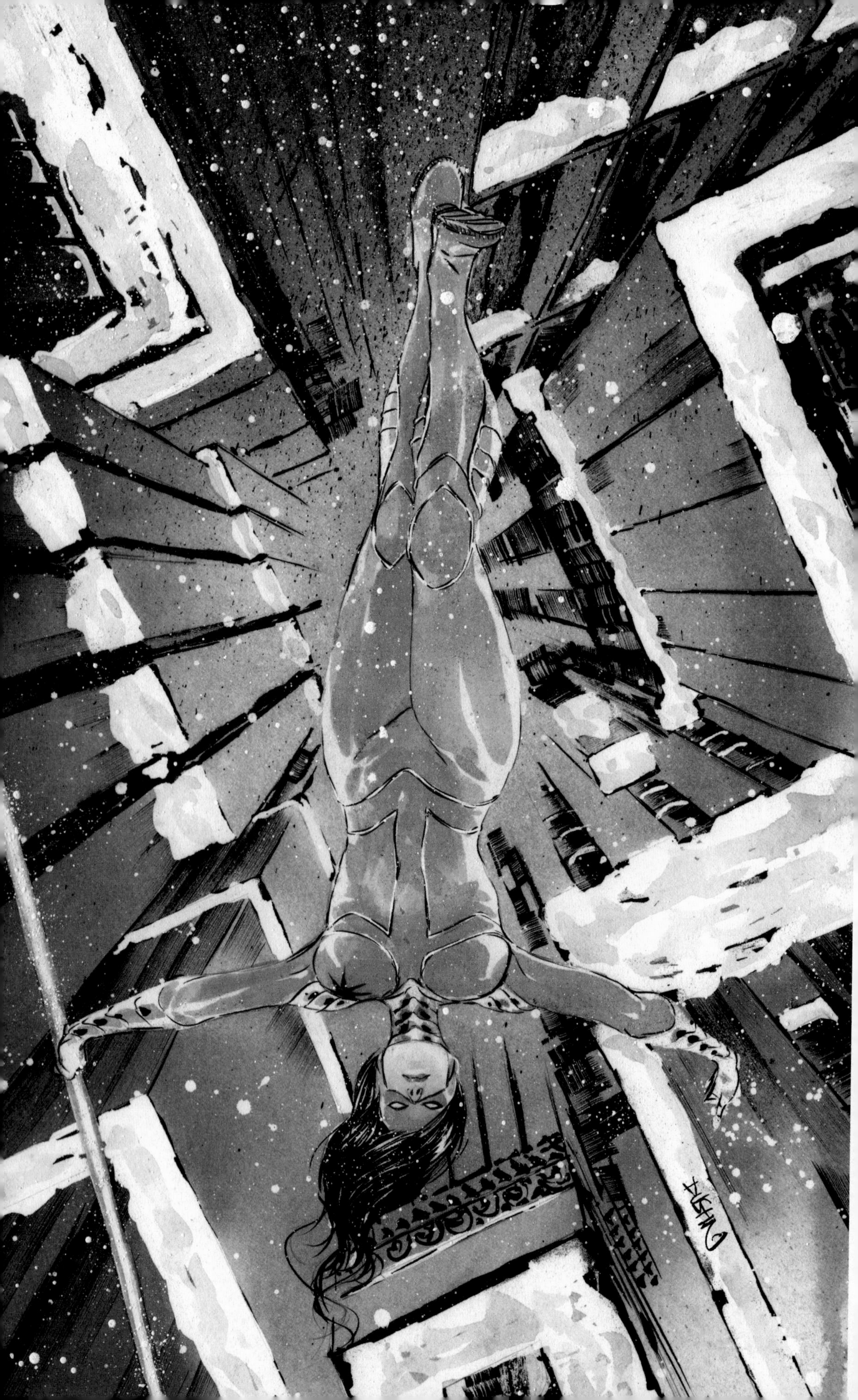

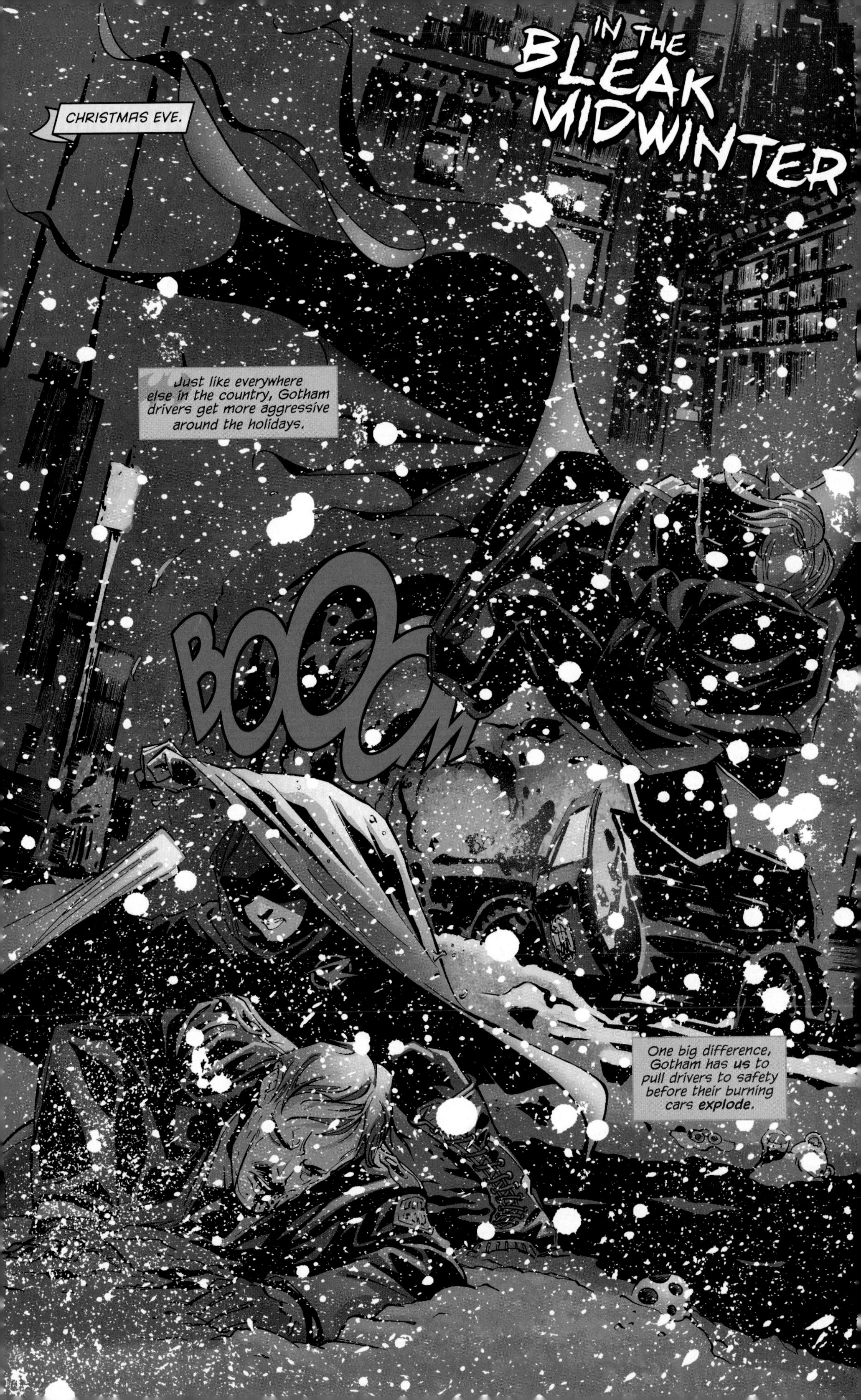
IN THE BLEAK MIDWINTER
CHRISTMAS EVE.
Just like everywhere else in the country, Gotham drivers get more aggressive around the holidays.
BOOOM
One big difference, Gotham has us to pull drivers to safety before their burning cars explode.

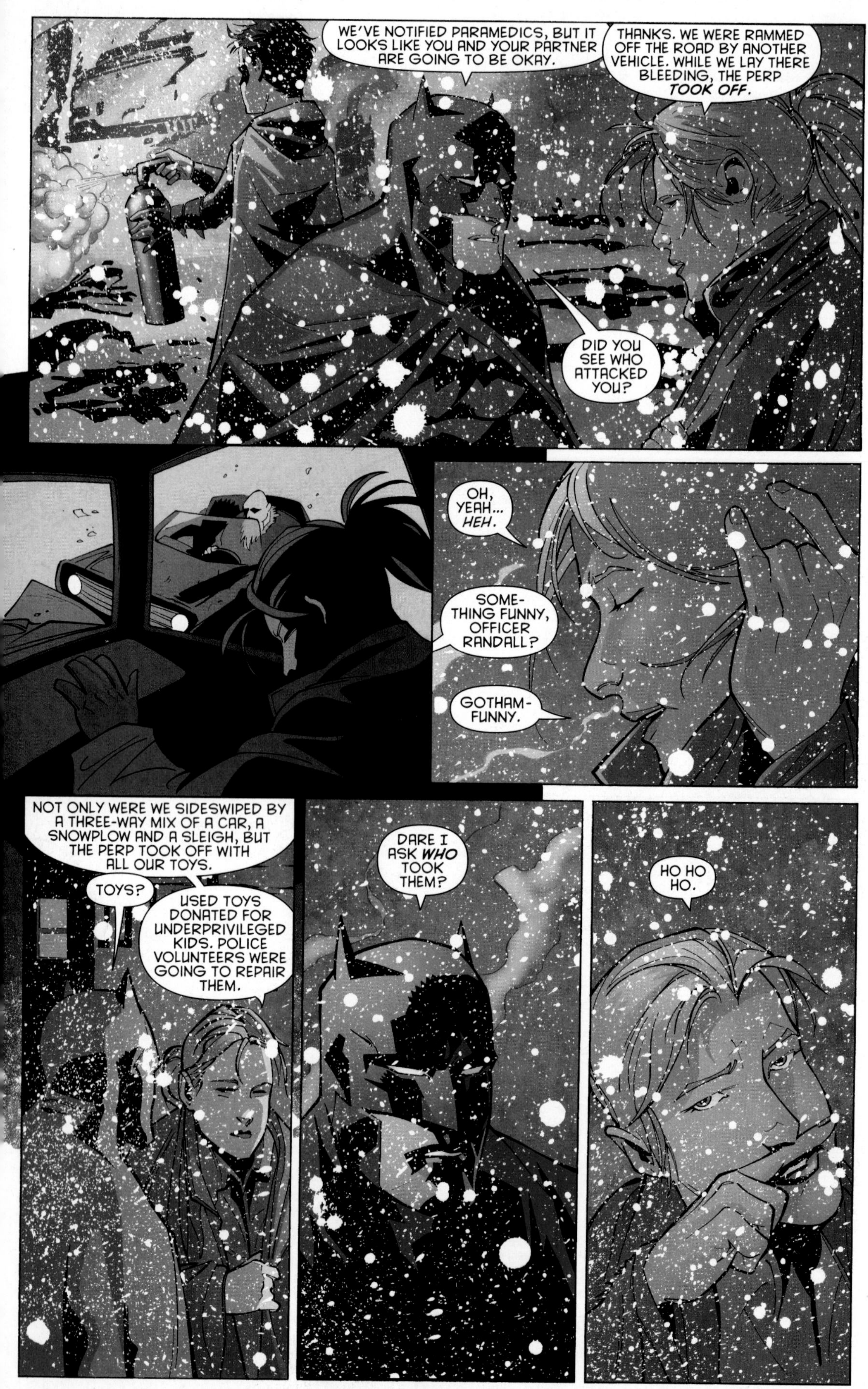
WE'VE NOTIFIED PARAMEDICS, BUT IT LOOKS LIKE YOU AND YOUR PARTNER ARE GOING TO BE OKAY.
THANKS. WE WERE RAMMED OFF THE ROAD BY ANOTHER VEHICLE. WHILE WE LAY THERE BLEEDING, THE PERP *TOOK OFF*.
DID YOU SEE WHO ATTACKED YOU?
OH, YEAH... *HEH*.
SOME-THING FUNNY, OFFICER RANDALL?
GOTHAM-FUNNY.
NOT ONLY WERE WE SIDESWIPED BY A THREE-WAY MIX OF A CAR, A SNOWPLOW AND A SLEIGH, BUT THE PERP TOOK OFF WITH ALL OUR TOYS.
TOYS?
USED TOYS DONATED FOR UNDERPRIVILEGED KIDS. POLICE VOLUNTEERS WERE GOING TO REPAIR THEM.
DARE I ASK *WHO* TOOK THEM?
HO HO HO.

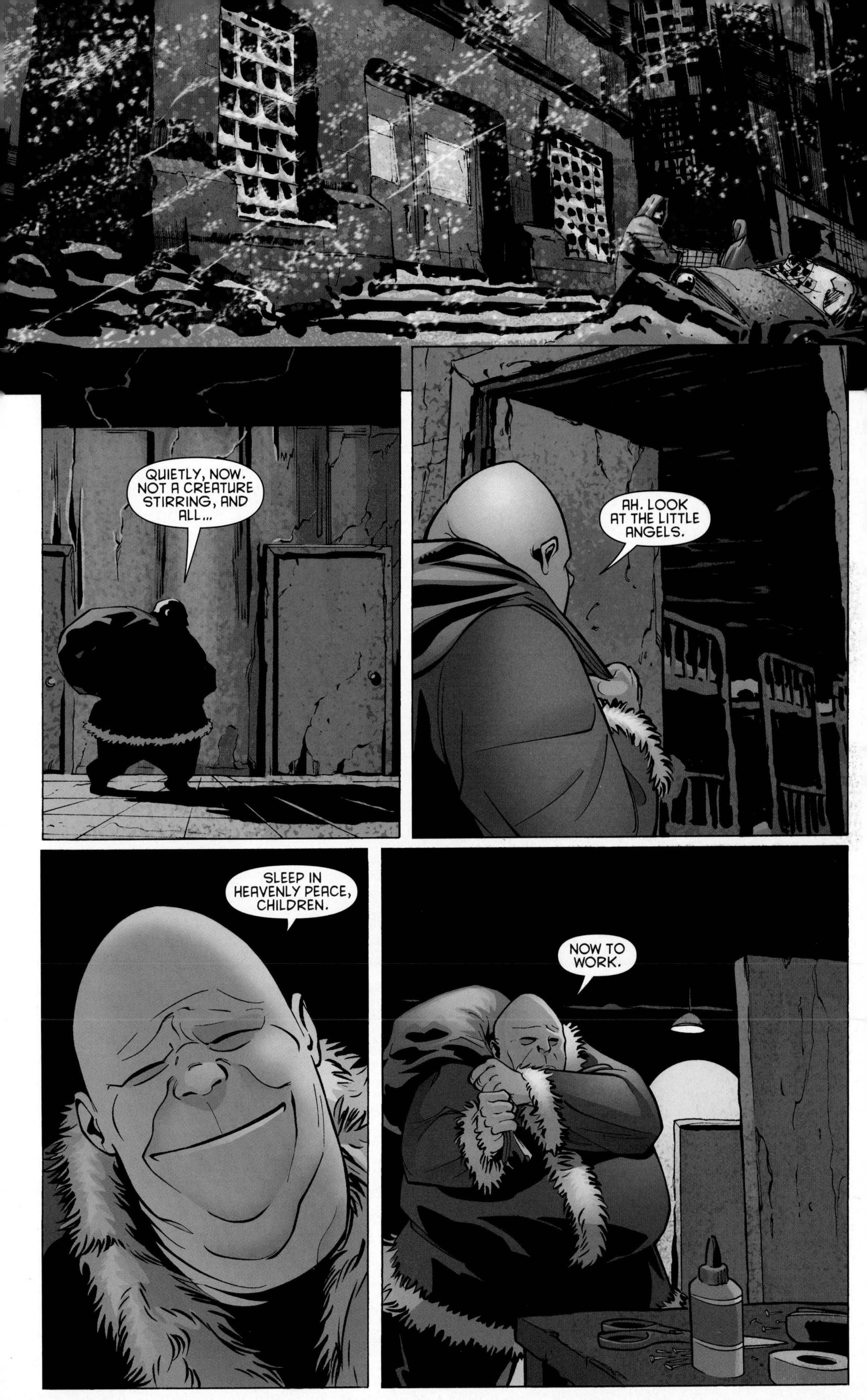
QUIETLY, NOW. NOT A CREATURE STIRRING, AND ALL...
AH. LOOK AT THE LITTLE ANGELS.
SLEEP IN HEAVENLY PEACE, CHILDREN.
NOW TO WORK.

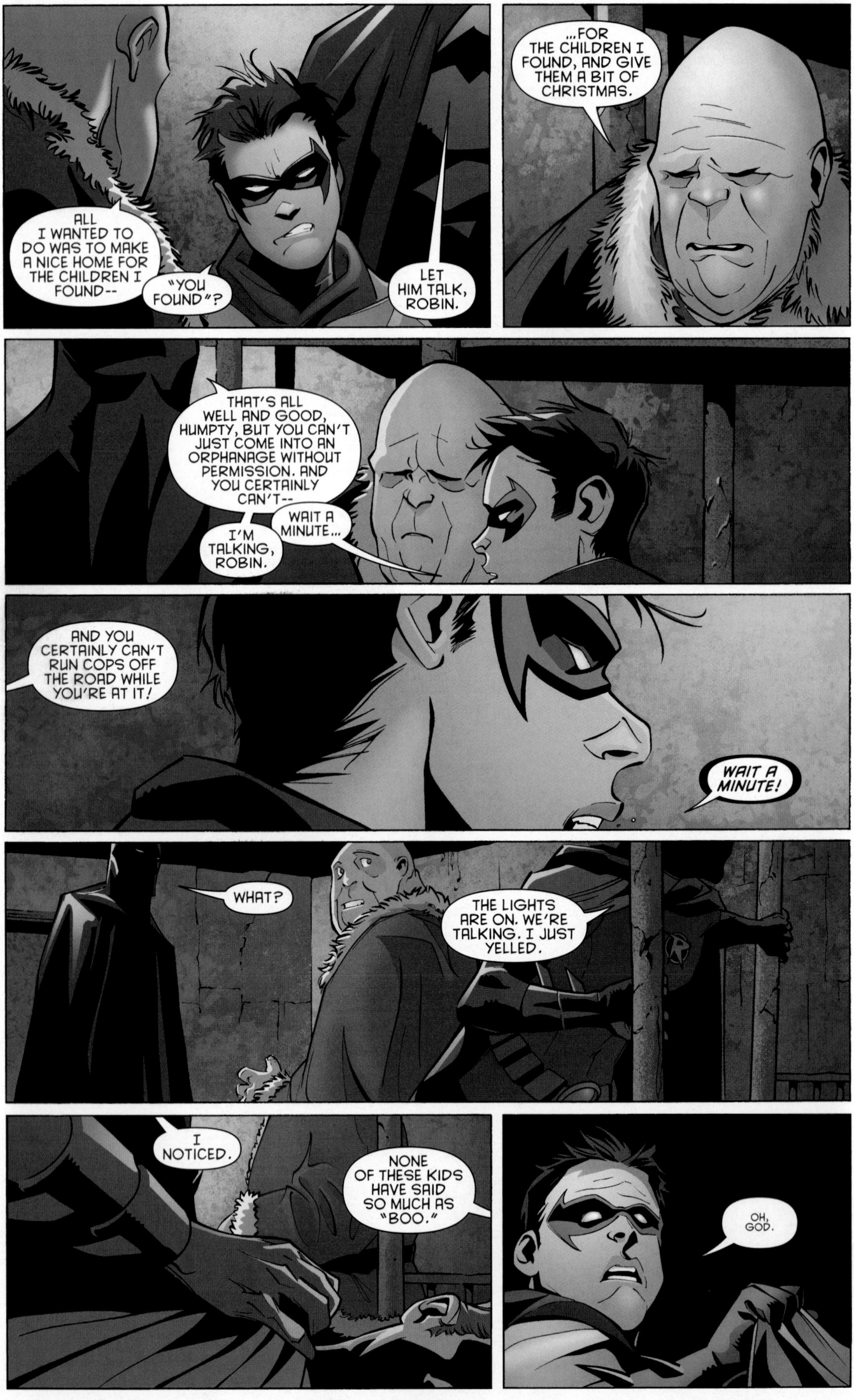
ALL I WANTED TO DO WAS TO MAKE A NICE HOME FOR THE CHILDREN I FOUND--
"YOU FOUND"?
LET HIM TALK, ROBIN.
...FOR THE CHILDREN I FOUND, AND GIVE THEM A BIT OF CHRISTMAS.
THAT'S ALL WELL AND GOOD, HUMPTY, BUT YOU CAN'T JUST COME INTO AN ORPHANAGE WITHOUT PERMISSION. AND YOU CERTAINLY CAN'T--
WAIT A MINUTE...
I'M TALKING, ROBIN.
AND YOU CERTAINLY CAN'T RUN COPS OFF THE ROAD WHILE YOU'RE AT IT!
WAIT A MINUTE!
WHAT?
THE LIGHTS ARE ON. WE'RE TALKING. I JUST YELLED.
I NOTICED.
NONE OF THESE KIDS HAVE SAID SO MUCH AS "BOO."
OH, GOD.

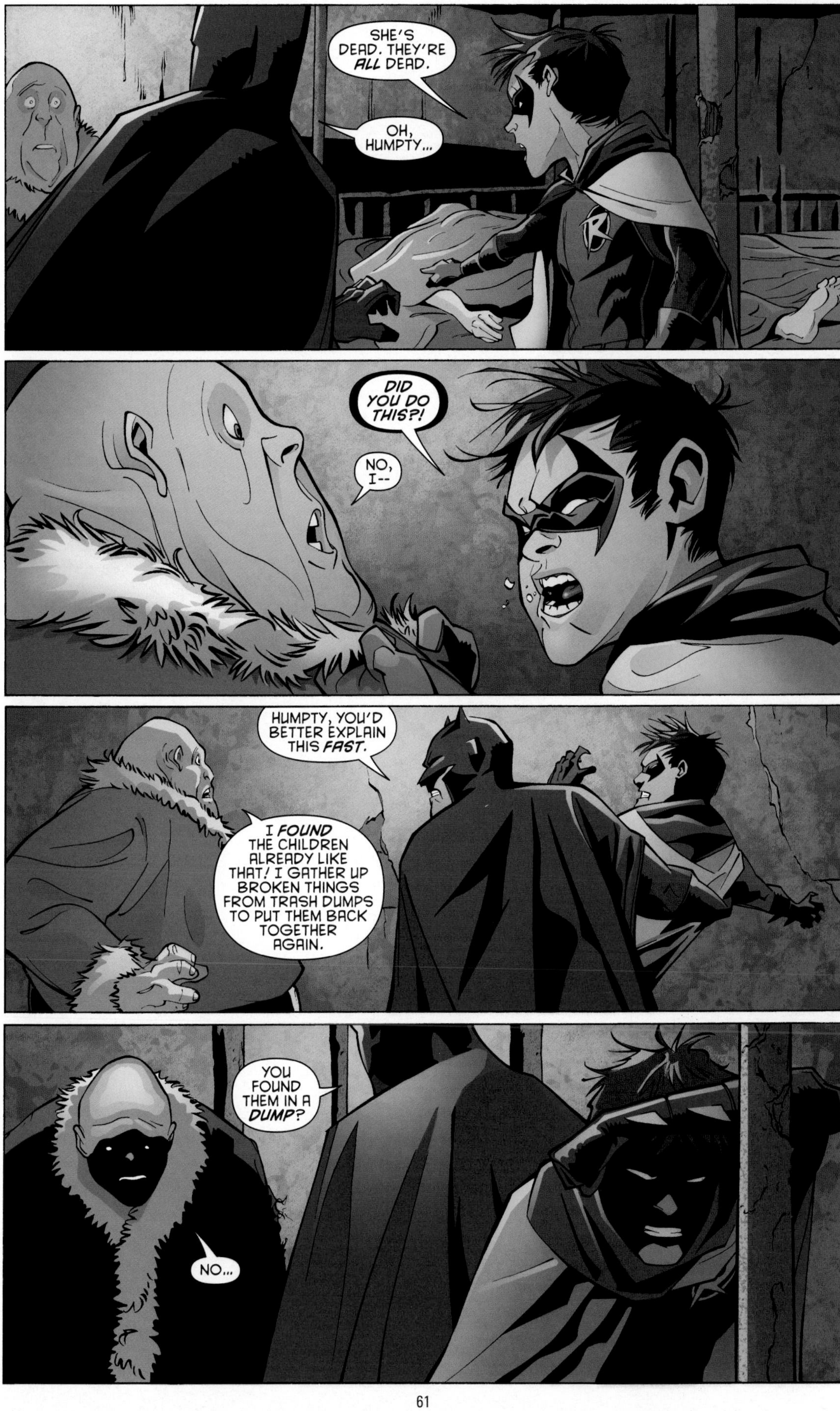
SHE'S DEAD. THEY'RE ALL DEAD.
OH, HUMPTY...
DID YOU DO THIS?!
NO, I--
HUMPTY, YOU'D BETTER EXPLAIN THIS FAST.
I FOUND THE CHILDREN ALREADY LIKE THAT! I GATHER UP BROKEN THINGS FROM TRASH DUMPS TO PUT THEM BACK TOGETHER AGAIN.
YOU FOUND THEM IN A DUMP?
NO...

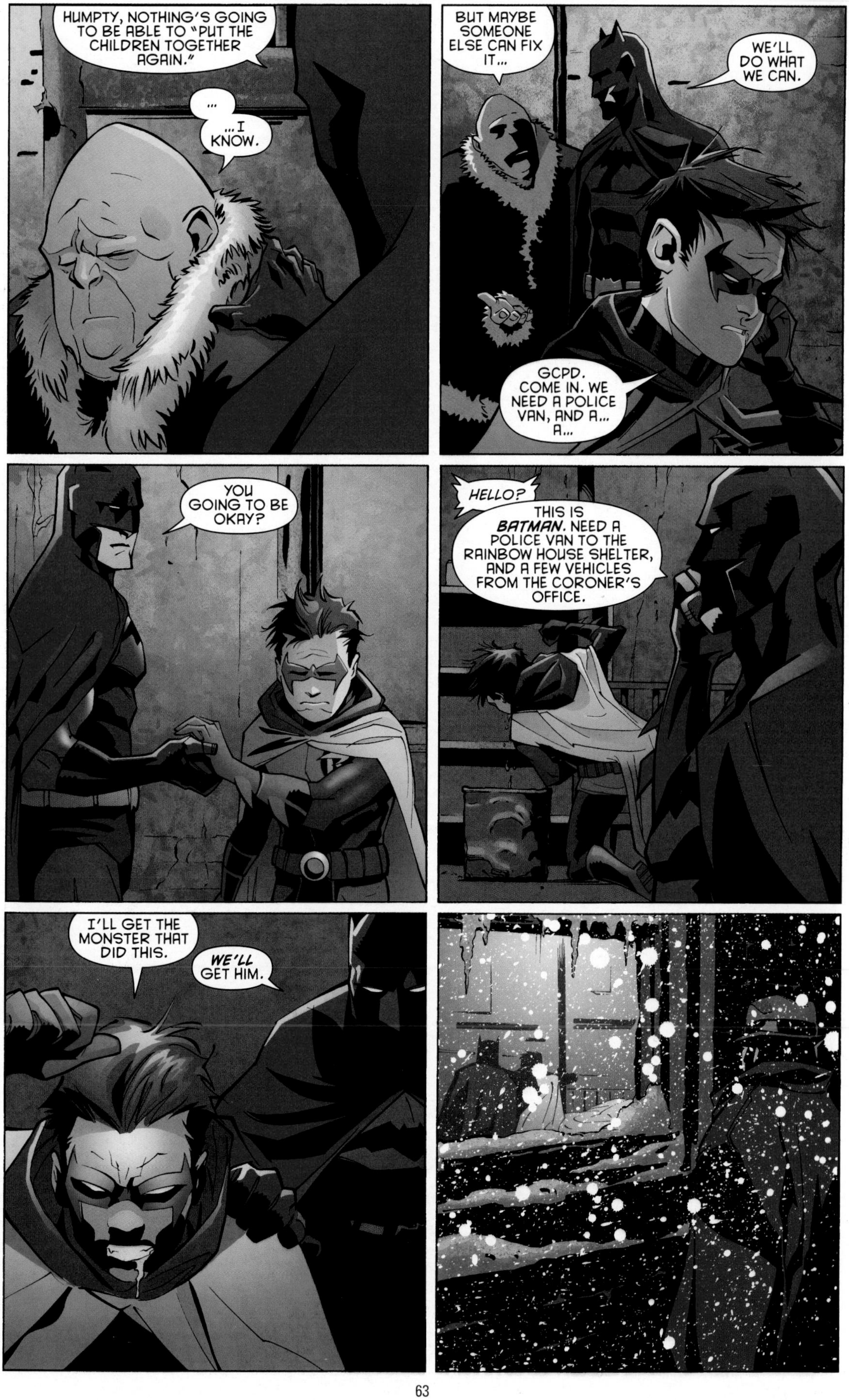
HUMPTY, NOTHING'S GOING TO BE ABLE TO "PUT THE CHILDREN TOGETHER AGAIN."
...
...I KNOW.
BUT MAYBE SOMEONE ELSE CAN FIX IT...
WE'LL DO WHAT WE CAN.
GCPD. COME IN. WE NEED A POLICE VAN, AND A... A...
YOU GOING TO BE OKAY?
HELLO?
THIS IS BATMAN. NEED A POLICE VAN TO THE RAINBOW HOUSE SHELTER, AND A FEW VEHICLES FROM THE CORONER'S OFFICE.
I'LL GET THE MONSTER THAT DID THIS.
WE'LL GET HIM.

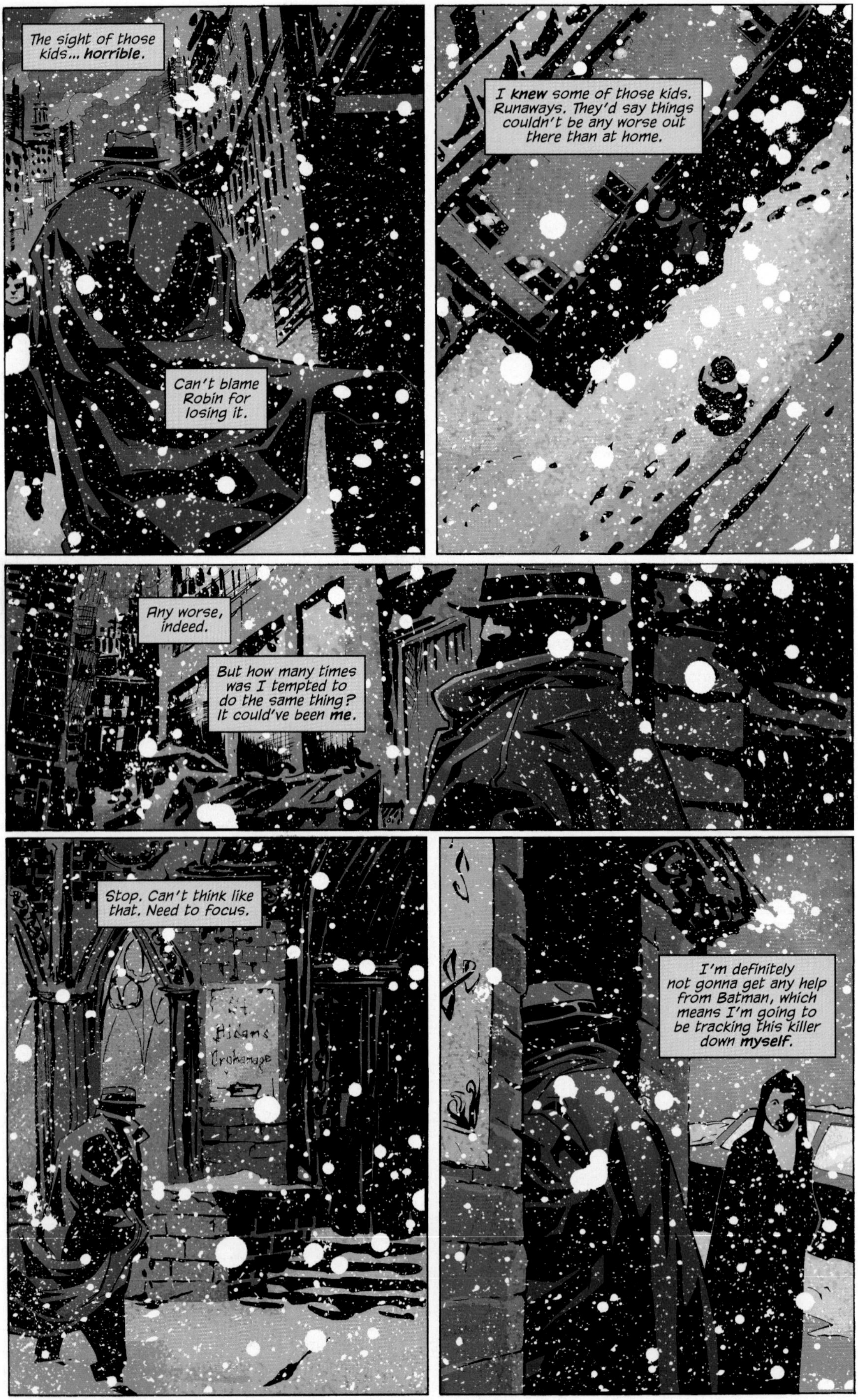
The sight of those kids... horrible.
Can't blame Robin for losing it.
I knew some of those kids. Runaways. They'd say things couldn't be any worse out there than at home.
Any worse, indeed.
But how many times was I tempted to do the same thing? It could've been me.
Stop. Can't think like that. Need to focus.
I'm definitely not gonna get any help from Batman, which means I'm going to be tracking this killer down myself.

SISTER AGNES?

SISTER AGNES, WHERE WERE YOU? IT'S ALMOST MIDNIGHT MASS.

COMING!

"Past Three o'clock, On a cold frosty morning..."

"...Past three o'clock, Good morrow masters all."

"Born is a baby Gentle as may be, Son of the Eternal Father supernal."

66

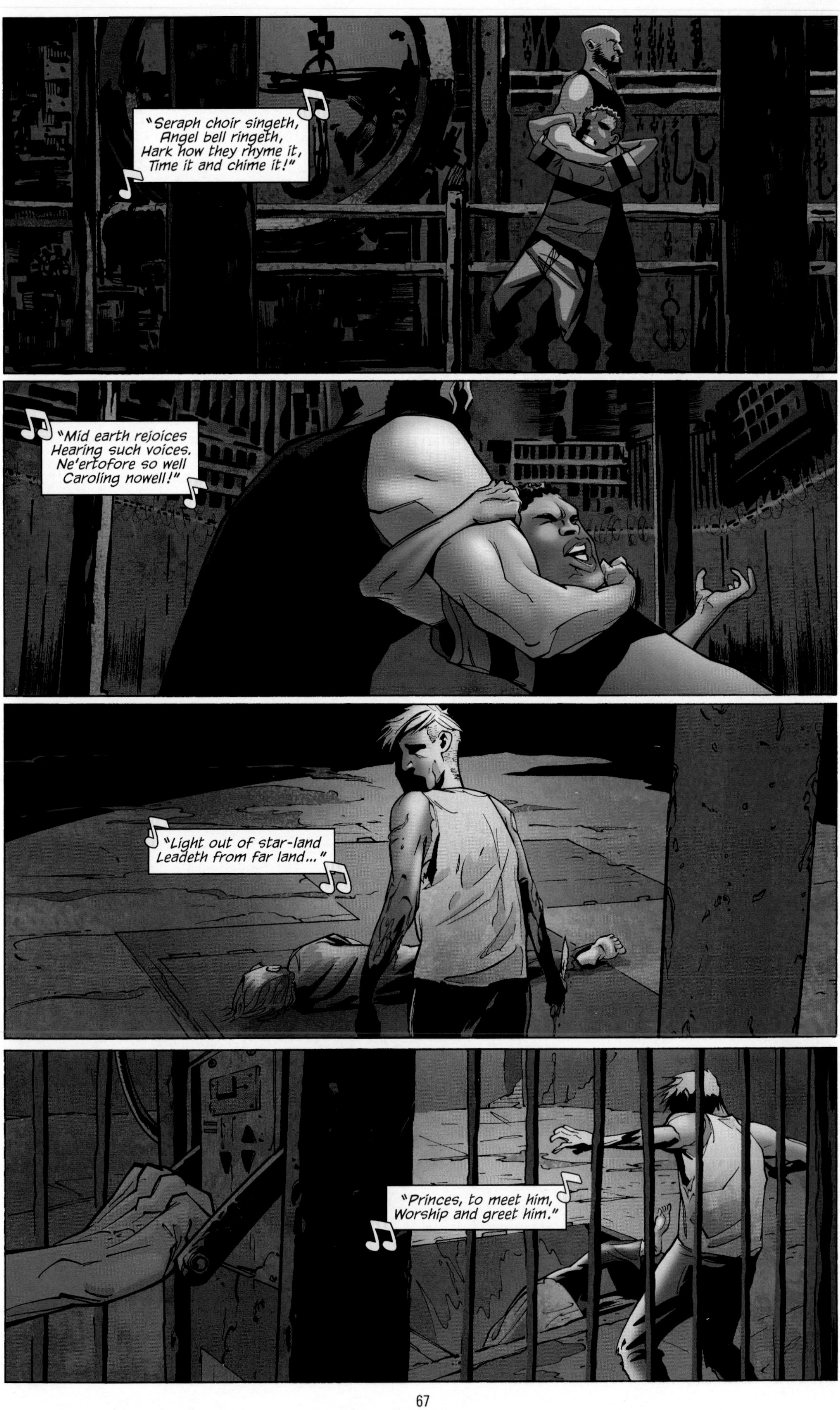
"Seraph choir singeth,
Angel bell ringeth,
Hark how they rhyme it,
Time it and chime it!"
"Mid earth rejoices
Hearing such voices.
Ne'ertofore so well
Caroling nowell!"
"Light out of star-land
Leadeth from far land..."
"Princes, to meet him,
Worship and greet him."

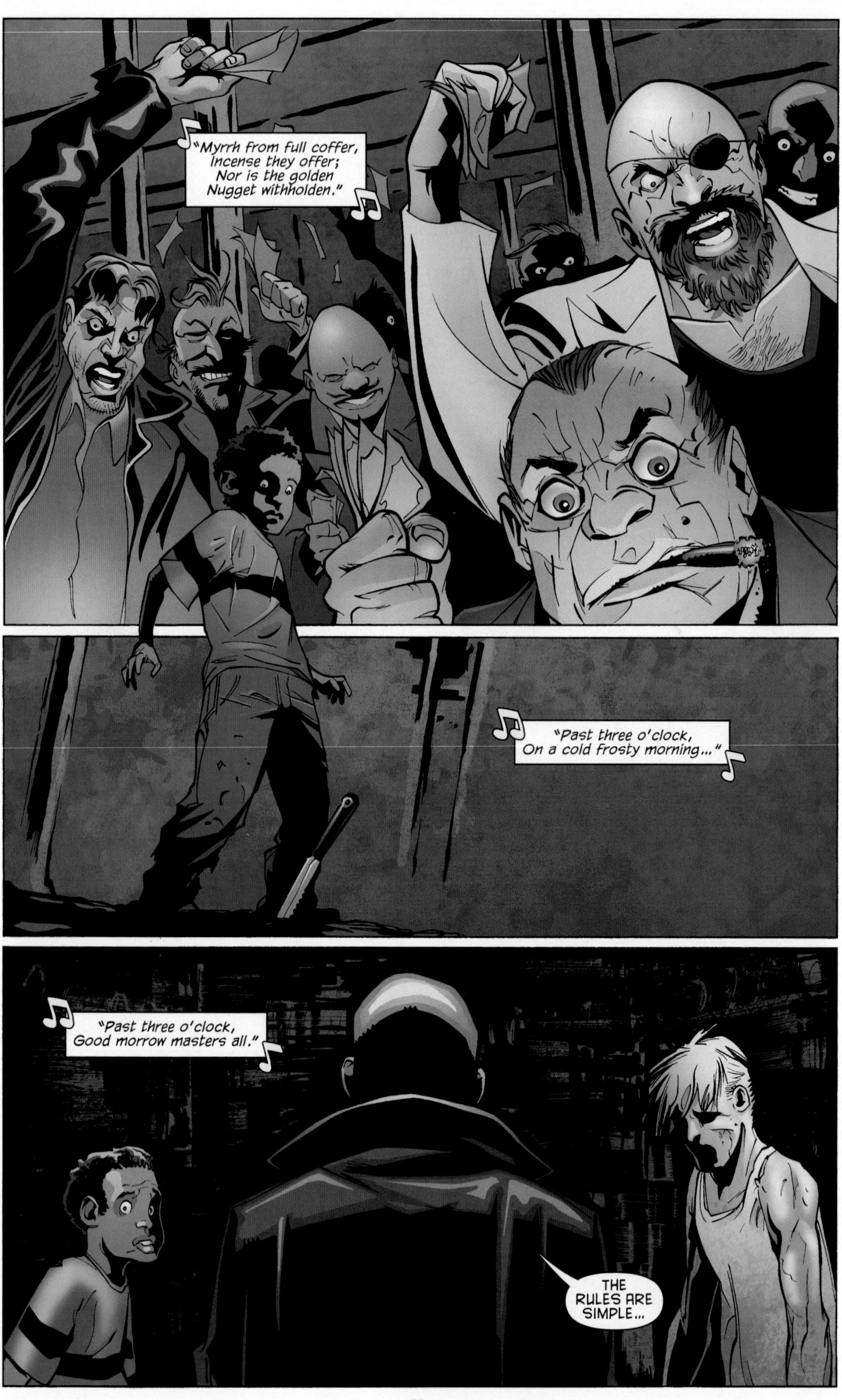
"Myrrh from full coffer,
Incense they offer;
Nor is the golden
Nugget withholden."
"Past three o'clock,
On a cold frosty morning..."
"Past three o'clock,
Good morrow masters all."
THE RULES ARE SIMPLE...

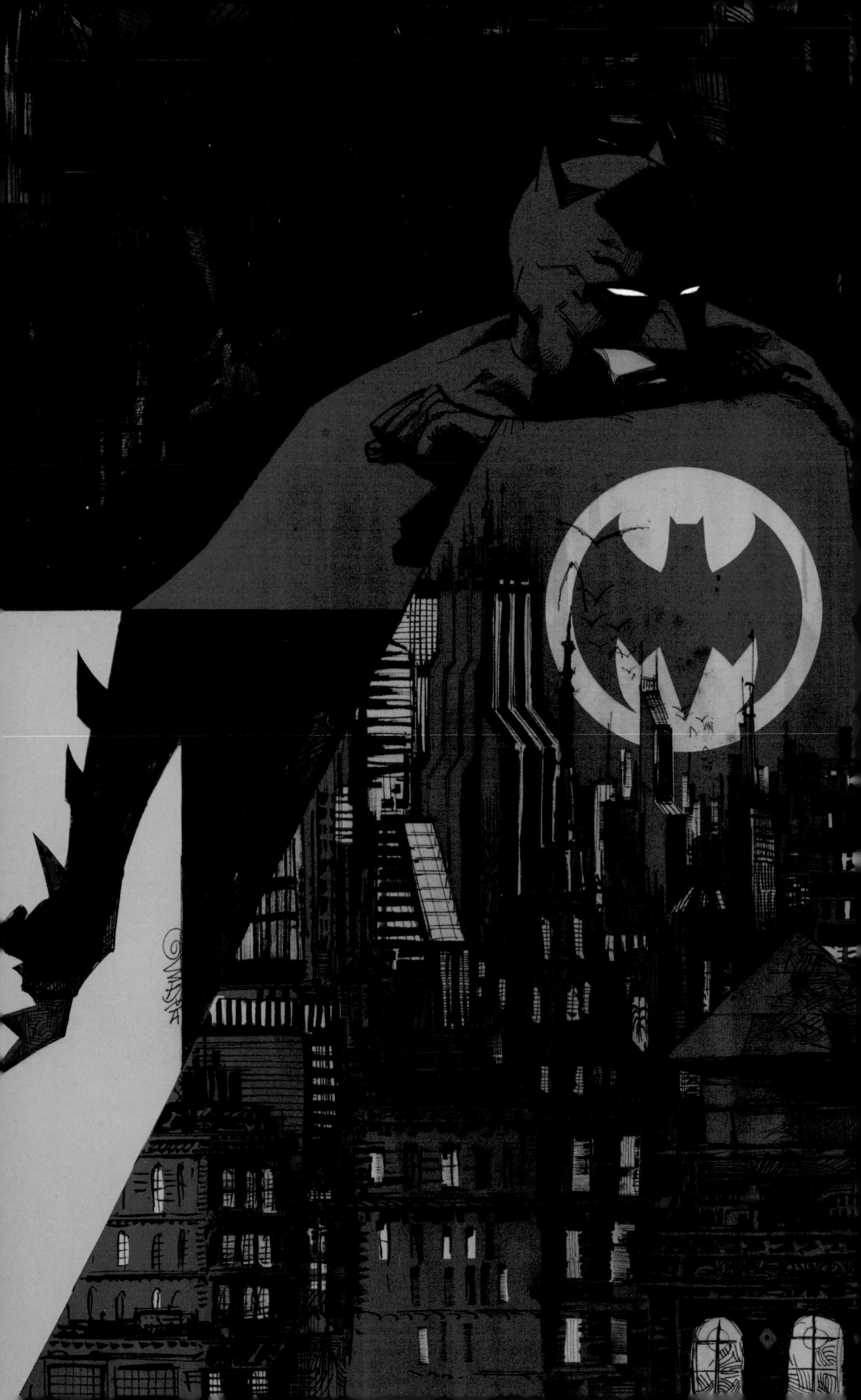

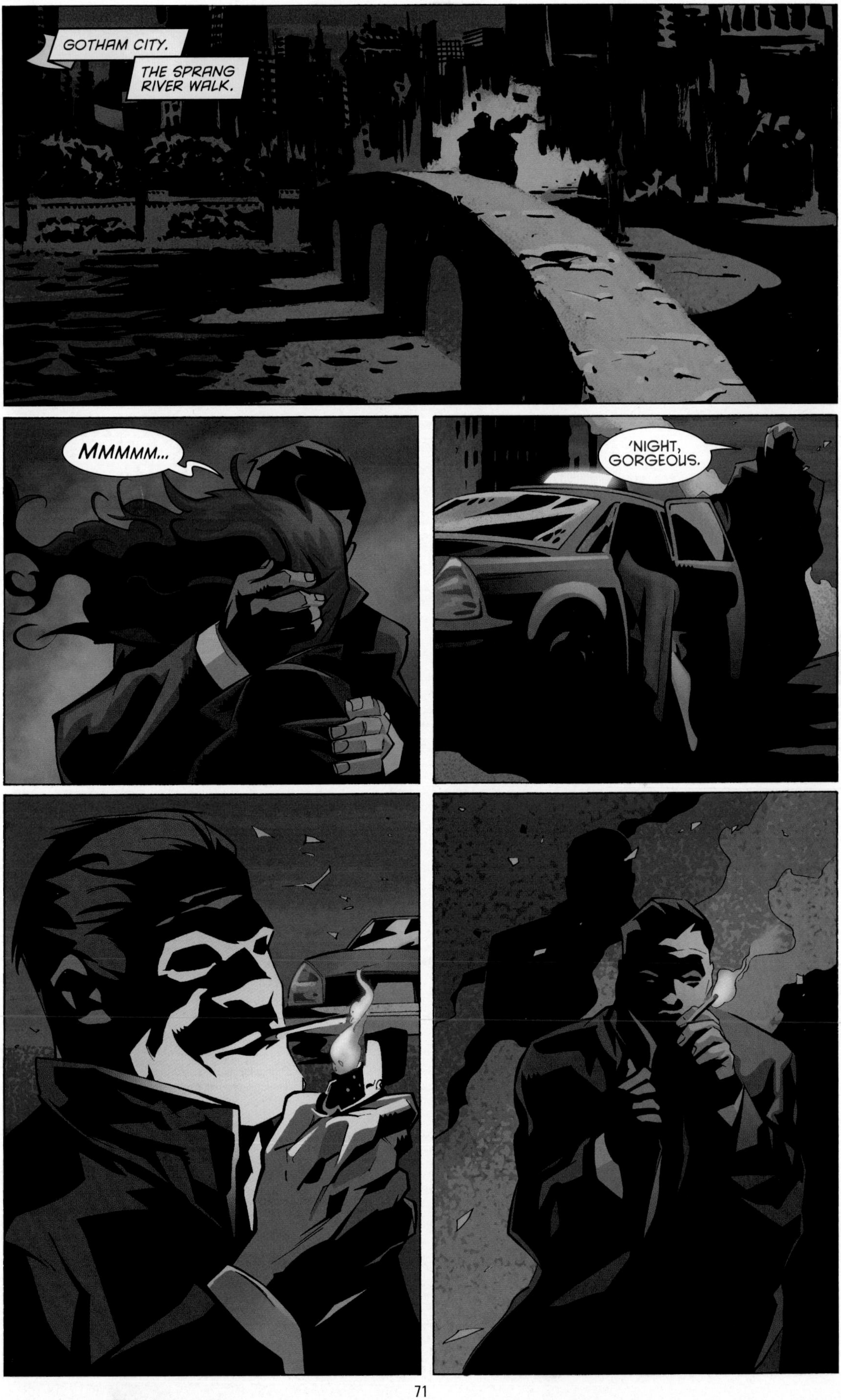
GOTHAM CITY.
THE SPRANG RIVER WALK.
MMMMM...
'NIGHT, GORGEOUS.

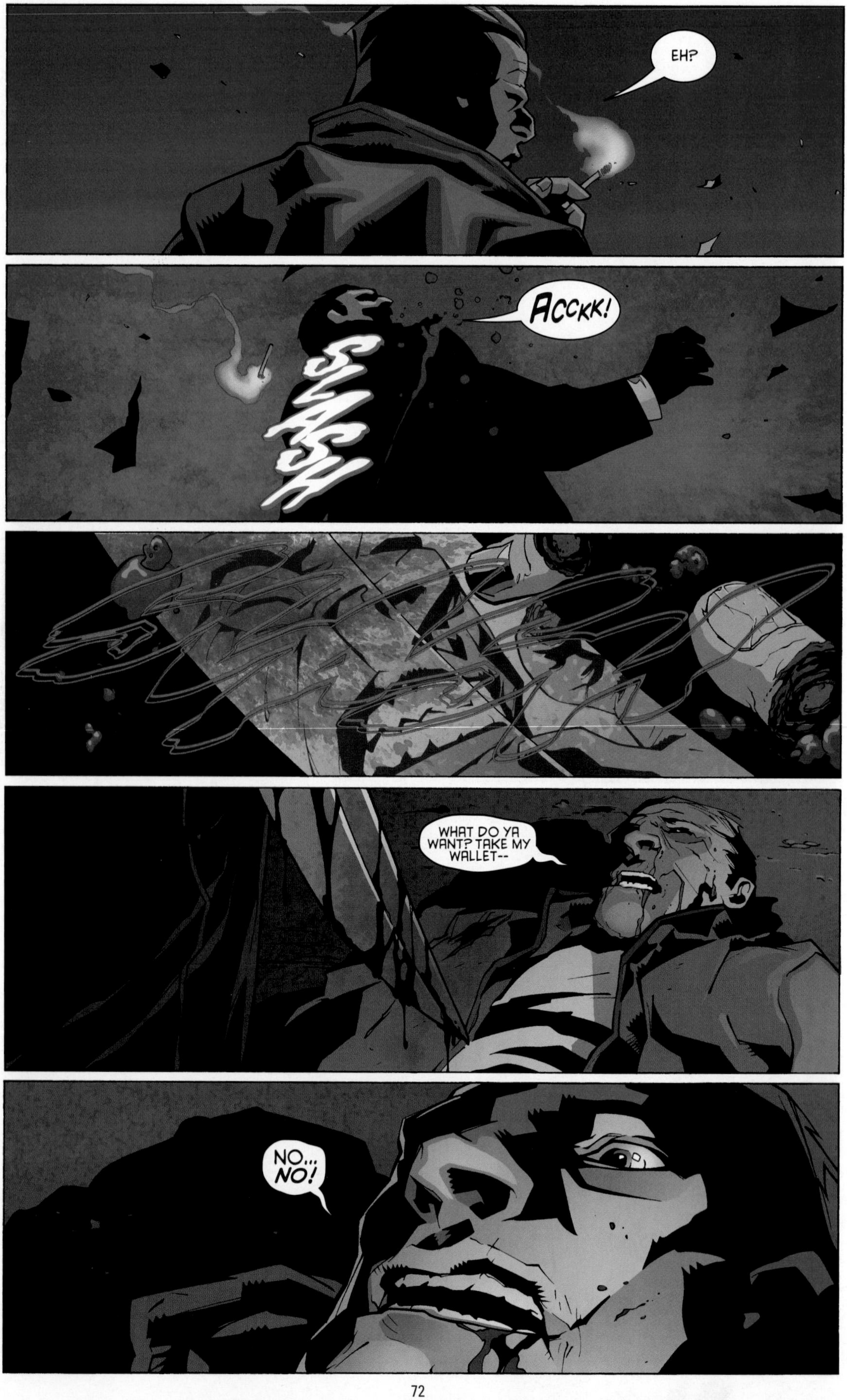
EH?
ACCKK!
SLASH
WHAT DO YA WANT? TAKE MY WALLET--
NO... NO!

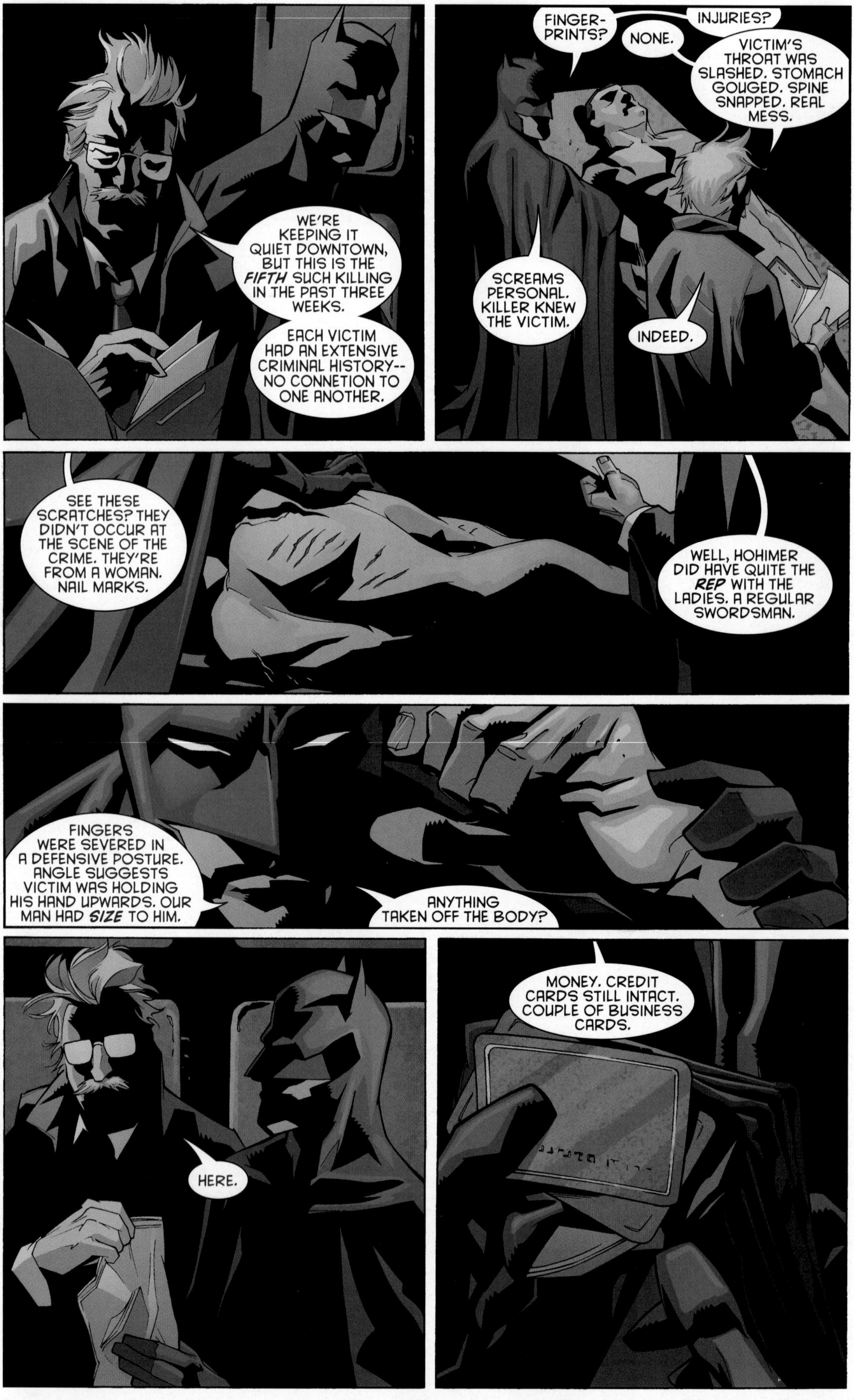
WE'RE KEEPING IT QUIET DOWNTOWN, BUT THIS IS THE FIFTH SUCH KILLING IN THE PAST THREE WEEKS.
EACH VICTIM HAD AN EXTENSIVE CRIMINAL HISTORY-- NO CONNETION TO ONE ANOTHER.
FINGER-PRINTS?
NONE.
INJURIES?
VICTIM'S THROAT WAS SLASHED. STOMACH GOUGED. SPINE SNAPPED. REAL MESS.
SCREAMS PERSONAL. KILLER KNEW THE VICTIM.
INDEED.
SEE THESE SCRATCHES? THEY DIDN'T OCCUR AT THE SCENE OF THE CRIME. THEY'RE FROM A WOMAN. NAIL MARKS.
WELL, HOHIMER DID HAVE QUITE THE REP WITH THE LADIES. A REGULAR SWORDSMAN.
FINGERS WERE SEVERED IN A DEFENSIVE POSTURE. ANGLE SUGGESTS VICTIM WAS HOLDING HIS HAND UPWARDS. OUR MAN HAD SIZE TO HIM.
ANYTHING TAKEN OFF THE BODY?
HERE.
MONEY. CREDIT CARDS STILL INTACT. COUPLE OF BUSINESS CARDS.

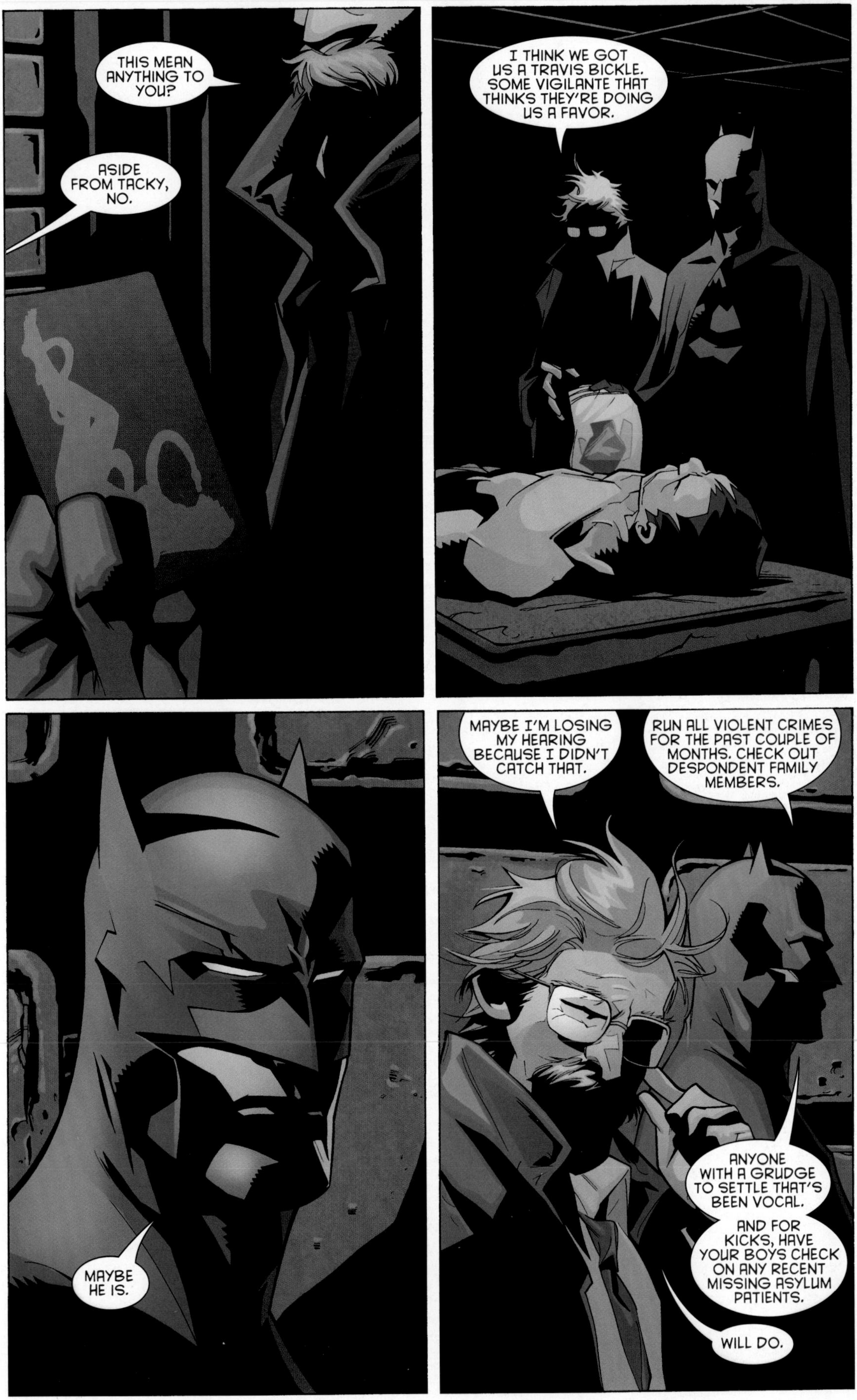
THIS MEAN ANYTHING TO YOU?
ASIDE FROM TACKY, NO.
I THINK WE GOT US A TRAVIS BICKLE. SOME VIGILANTE THAT THINKS THEY'RE DOING US A FAVOR.
MAYBE HE IS.
MAYBE I'M LOSING MY HEARING BECAUSE I DIDN'T CATCH THAT.
RUN ALL VIOLENT CRIMES FOR THE PAST COUPLE OF MONTHS. CHECK OUT DESPONDENT FAMILY MEMBERS.
ANYONE WITH A GRUDGE TO SETTLE THAT'S BEEN VOCAL.
AND FOR KICKS, HAVE YOUR BOYS CHECK ON ANY RECENT MISSING ASYLUM PATIENTS.
WILL DO.

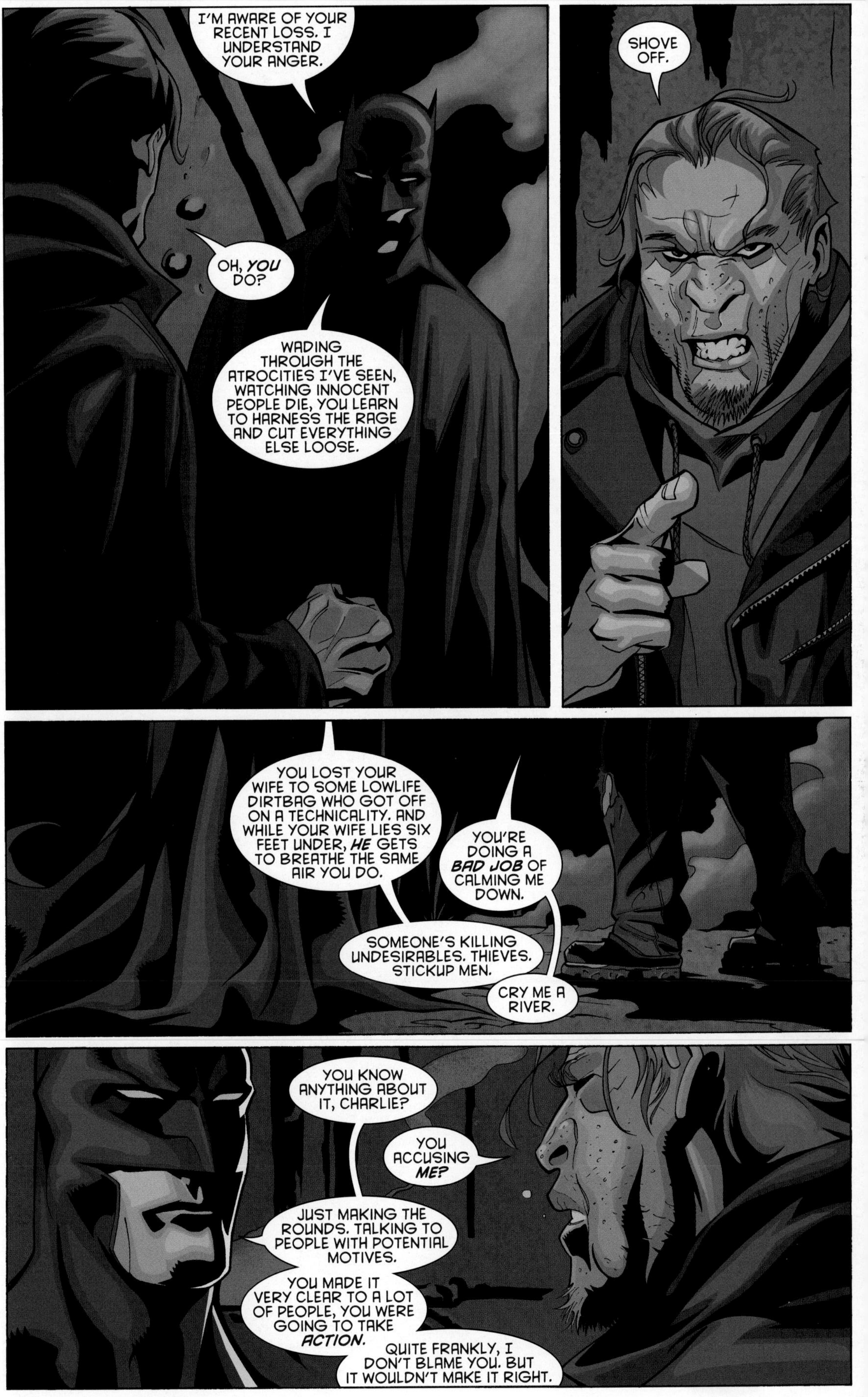
I'M AWARE OF YOUR RECENT LOSS. I UNDERSTAND YOUR ANGER.
OH, *YOU* DO?
WADING THROUGH THE ATROCITIES I'VE SEEN, WATCHING INNOCENT PEOPLE DIE, YOU LEARN TO HARNESS THE RAGE AND CUT EVERYTHING ELSE LOOSE.
SHOVE OFF.
YOU LOST YOUR WIFE TO SOME LOWLIFE DIRTBAG WHO GOT OFF ON A TECHNICALITY. AND WHILE YOUR WIFE LIES SIX FEET UNDER, *HE* GETS TO BREATHE THE SAME AIR YOU DO.
YOU'RE DOING A *BAD JOB* OF CALMING ME DOWN.
SOMEONE'S KILLING UNDESIRABLES. THIEVES. STICKUP MEN.
CRY ME A RIVER.
YOU KNOW ANYTHING ABOUT IT, CHARLIE?
YOU ACCUSING *ME?*
JUST MAKING THE ROUNDS. TALKING TO PEOPLE WITH POTENTIAL MOTIVES.
YOU MADE IT VERY CLEAR TO A LOT OF PEOPLE, YOU WERE GOING TO TAKE *ACTION.*
QUITE FRANKLY, I DON'T BLAME YOU. BUT IT WOULDN'T MAKE IT RIGHT.

YOU WANNA KNOW THE *TRUTH?* I GOT A TWELVE-YEAR-OLD GIRL WHO'S GONE THROUGH TOO MUCH GRIEF AS IT IS.

I DO ANOTHER STRETCH IN BLACKGATE AND SHE'LL TURN TO DANCING IN CLUBS...AND I *CAN'T* HAVE THAT.

AND AS MUCH AS I'D GET OFF PUTTING A CAP IN SOME LOWLIFE'S HEAD, IT AIN'T GONNA BRING KAREN BACK.

SO TAKE ME AT MY WORD OR DO WHAT YOU GOTTA DO.

GO.

THAT'S IT?

YOU'RE TELLING THE TRUTH. I'VE BEEN MONITORING YOUR HEART RATE.

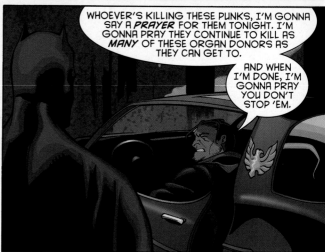

WHOEVER'S KILLING THESE PUNKS, I'M GONNA SAY A *PRAYER* FOR THEM TONIGHT. I'M GONNA PRAY THEY CONTINUE TO KILL AS *MANY* OF THESE ORGAN DONORS AS THEY CAN GET TO.

AND WHEN I'M DONE, I'M GONNA PRAY YOU DON'T STOP 'EM.

Sometimes the lines get blurred. Sometimes the only difference between you and them is the mask and cape.

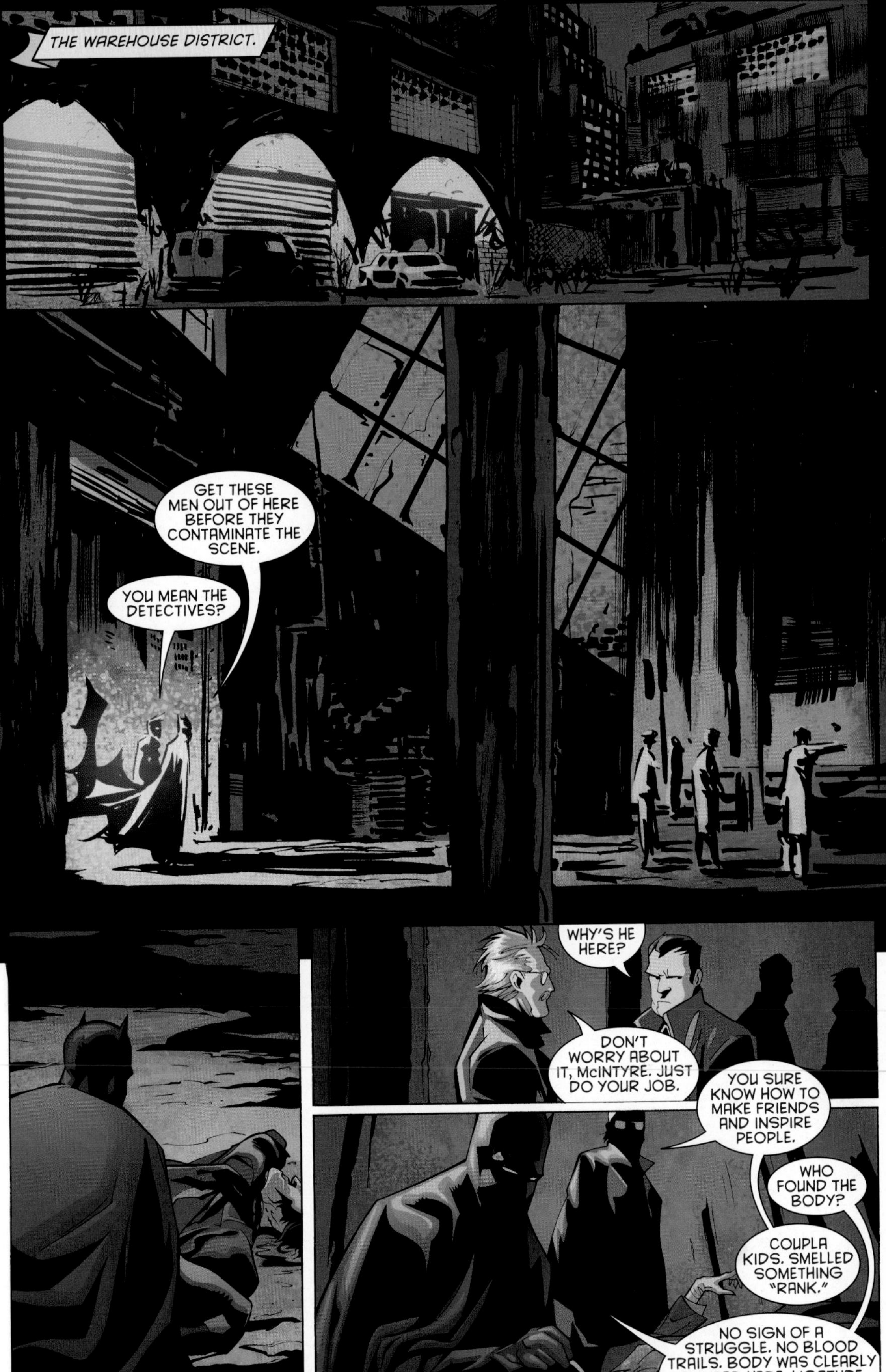
THE WAREHOUSE DISTRICT.
GET THESE MEN OUT OF HERE BEFORE THEY CONTAMINATE THE SCENE.
YOU MEAN THE DETECTIVES?
WHY'S HE HERE?
DON'T WORRY ABOUT IT, McINTYRE. JUST DO YOUR JOB.
YOU SURE KNOW HOW TO MAKE FRIENDS AND INSPIRE PEOPLE.
WHO FOUND THE BODY?
COUPLA KIDS. SMELLED SOMETHING "RANK."
NO SIGN OF A STRUGGLE. NO BLOOD TRAILS. BODY WAS CLEARLY DUMPED HERE. LIGATURE MARKS ON THE WRISTS SUGGEST HANDCUFFS.

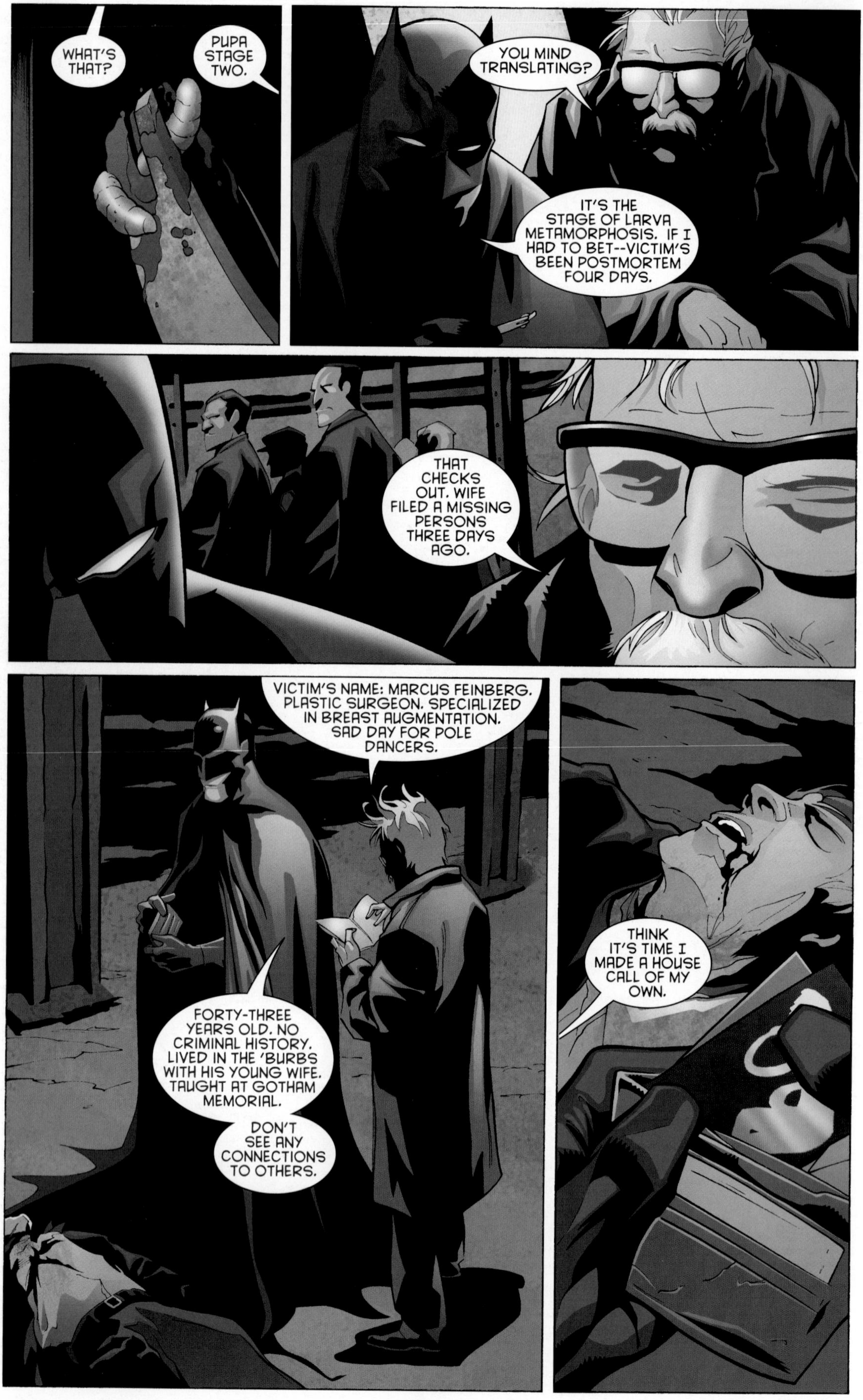
WHAT'S THAT?
PUPA STAGE TWO.
YOU MIND TRANSLATING?
IT'S THE STAGE OF LARVA METAMORPHOSIS. IF I HAD TO BET--VICTIM'S BEEN POSTMORTEM FOUR DAYS.
THAT CHECKS OUT. WIFE FILED A MISSING PERSONS THREE DAYS AGO.
VICTIM'S NAME: MARCUS FEINBERG. PLASTIC SURGEON. SPECIALIZED IN BREAST AUGMENTATION. SAD DAY FOR POLE DANCERS.
FORTY-THREE YEARS OLD. NO CRIMINAL HISTORY. LIVED IN THE 'BURBS WITH HIS YOUNG WIFE. TAUGHT AT GOTHAM MEMORIAL.
DON'T SEE ANY CONNECTIONS TO OTHERS.
THINK IT'S TIME I MADE A HOUSE CALL OF MY OWN.

And then it came gift wrapped in a little black dress.

Also known as a Sex Goddess. The Pamela Anderson of her day.

BINGO.

I didn't recognize it before, but the image was now clear. The girl on the card was **Qetesh**--the Egyptian Goddess of goodness and beauty.

I'LL HAVE THE NUMBERS TRACED AND SEE IF ANYTHING OF INTEREST COMES UP.

With an address I had a solid starting point.

Held properly you could hear a pin drop a block away.

Only I wasn't listening for a pin. I was listening for a name.

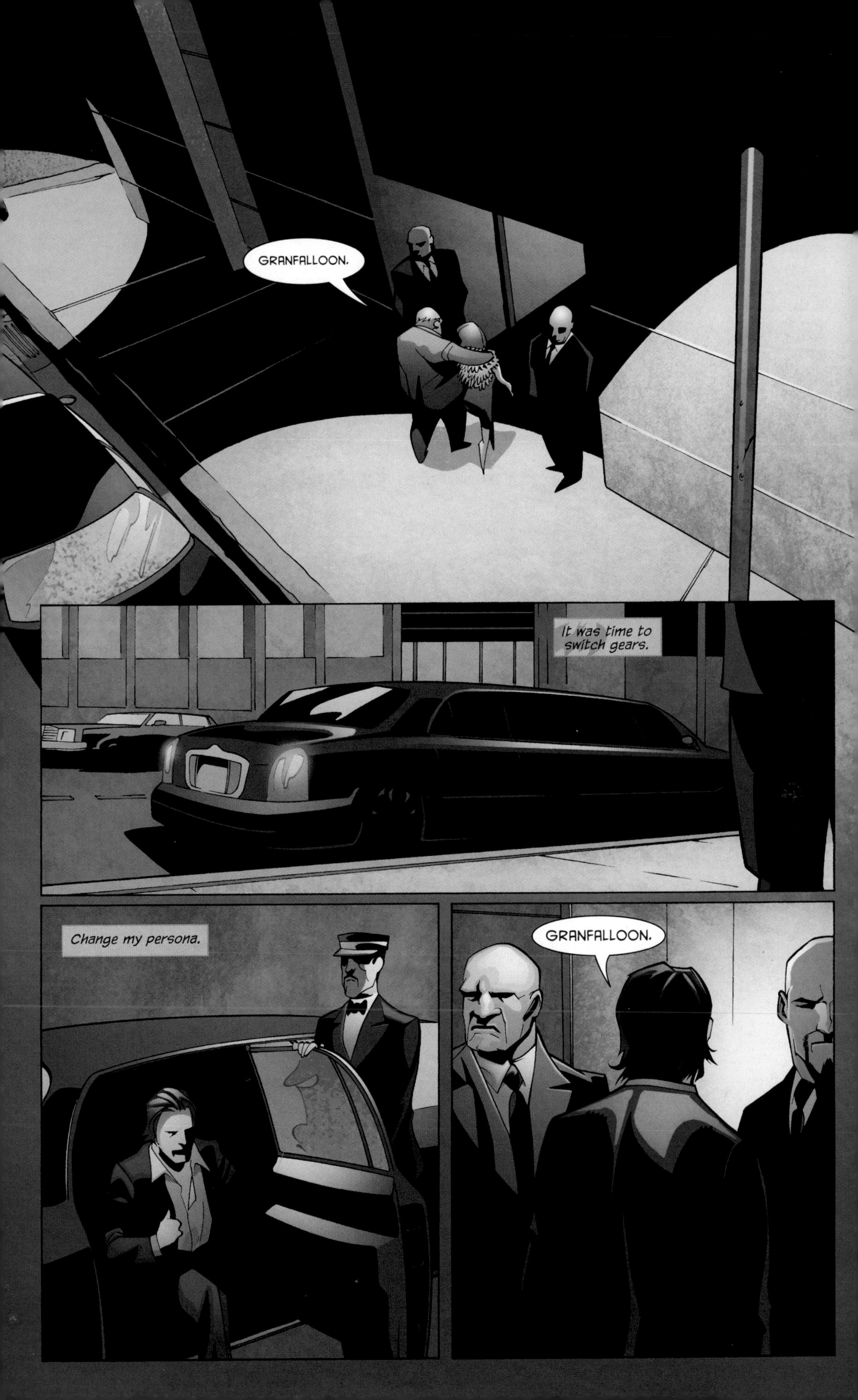
GRANFALLOON.
It was time to switch gears.
Change my persona.
GRANFALLOON.

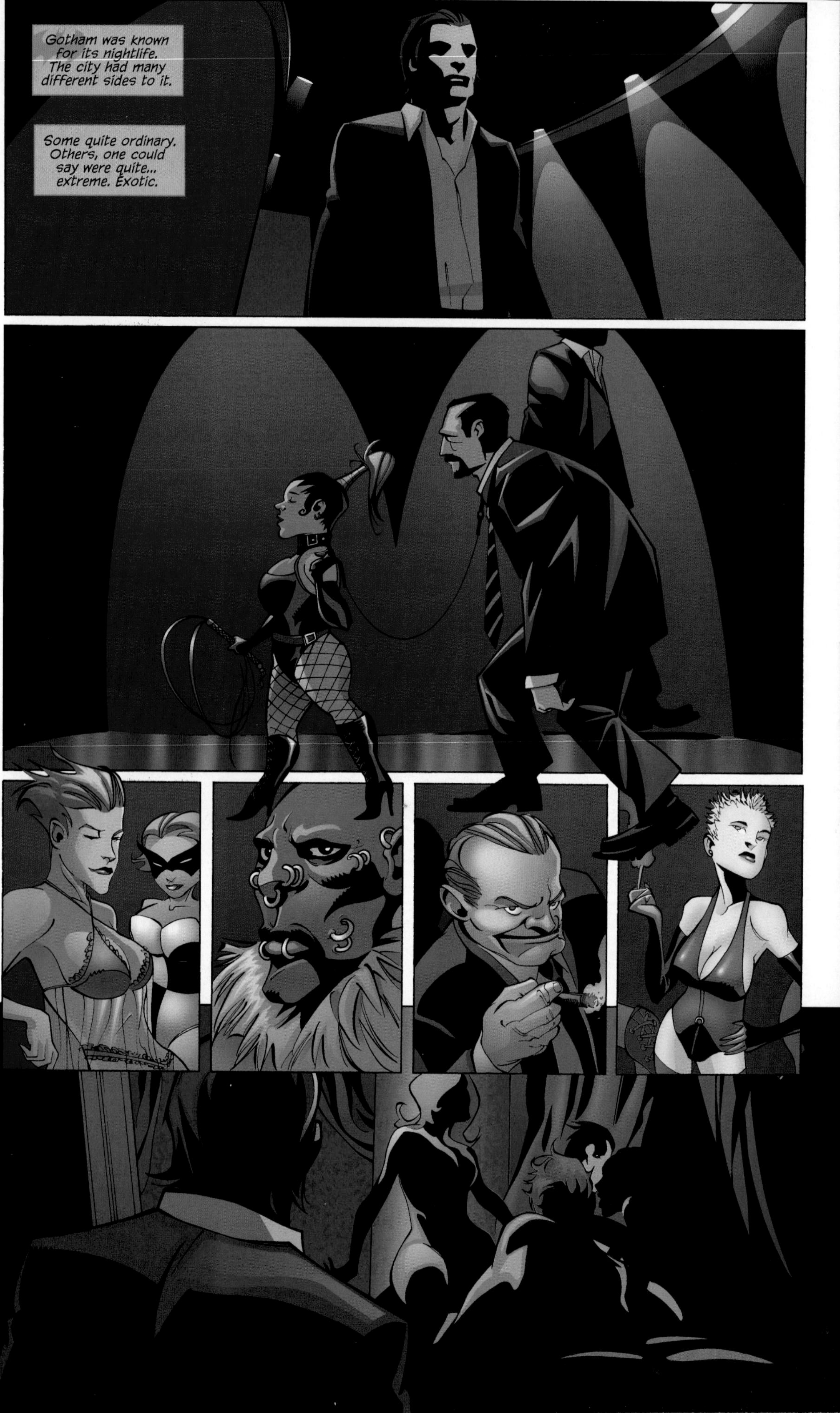
Gotham was known for its nightlife. The city had many different sides to it.
Some quite ordinary. Others, one could say were quite... extreme. Exotic.

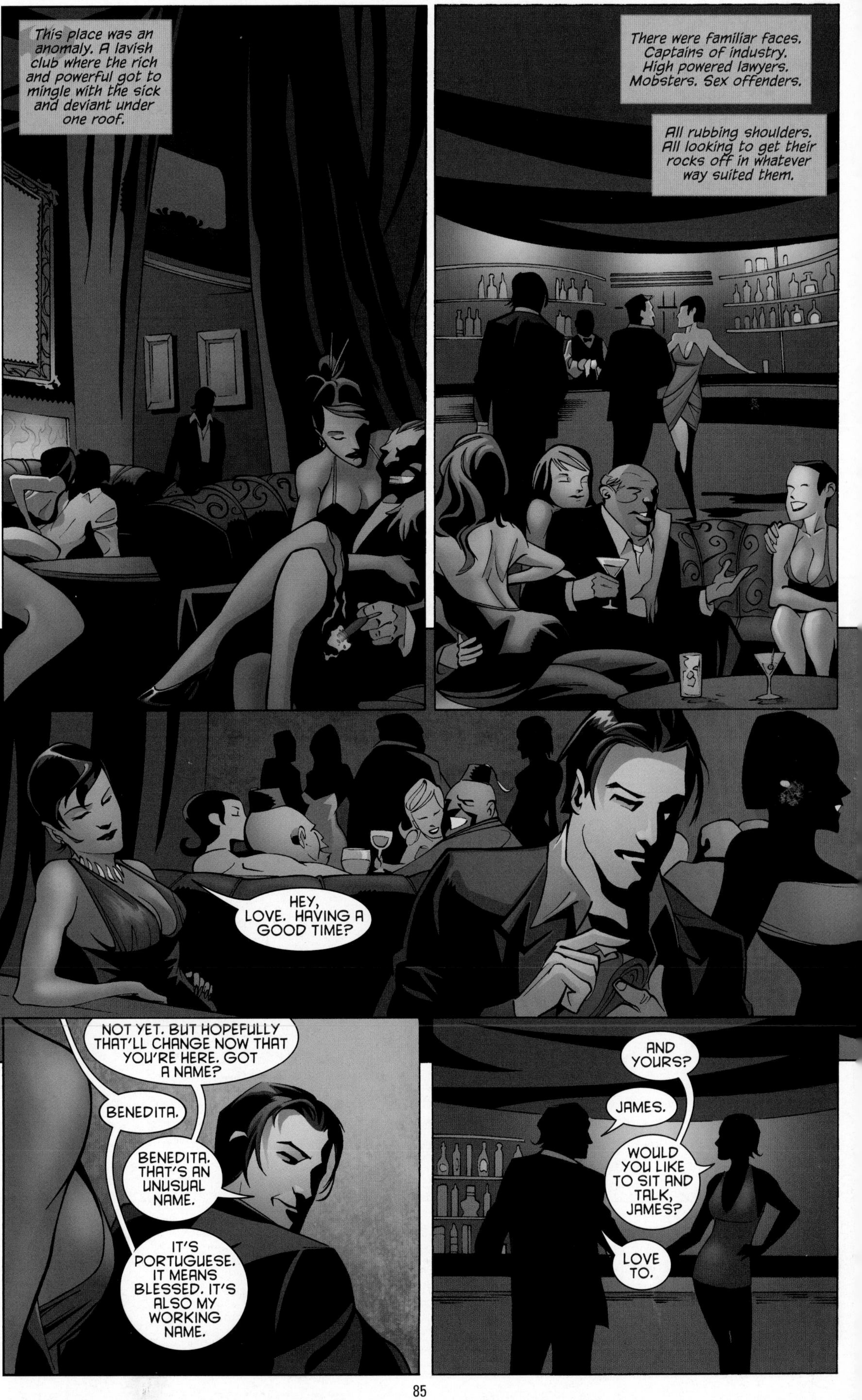
This place was an anomaly. A lavish club where the rich and powerful got to mingle with the sick and deviant under one roof.
There were familiar faces. Captains of industry. High powered lawyers. Mobsters. Sex offenders.
All rubbing shoulders. All looking to get their rocks off in whatever way suited them.
HEY, LOVE. HAVING A GOOD TIME?
NOT YET. BUT HOPEFULLY THAT'LL CHANGE NOW THAT YOU'RE HERE. GOT A NAME?
BENEDITA.
BENEDITA. THAT'S AN UNUSUAL NAME.
IT'S PORTUGUESE. IT MEANS BLESSED. IT'S ALSO MY WORKING NAME.
AND YOURS?
JAMES.
WOULD YOU LIKE TO SIT AND TALK, JAMES?
LOVE TO.

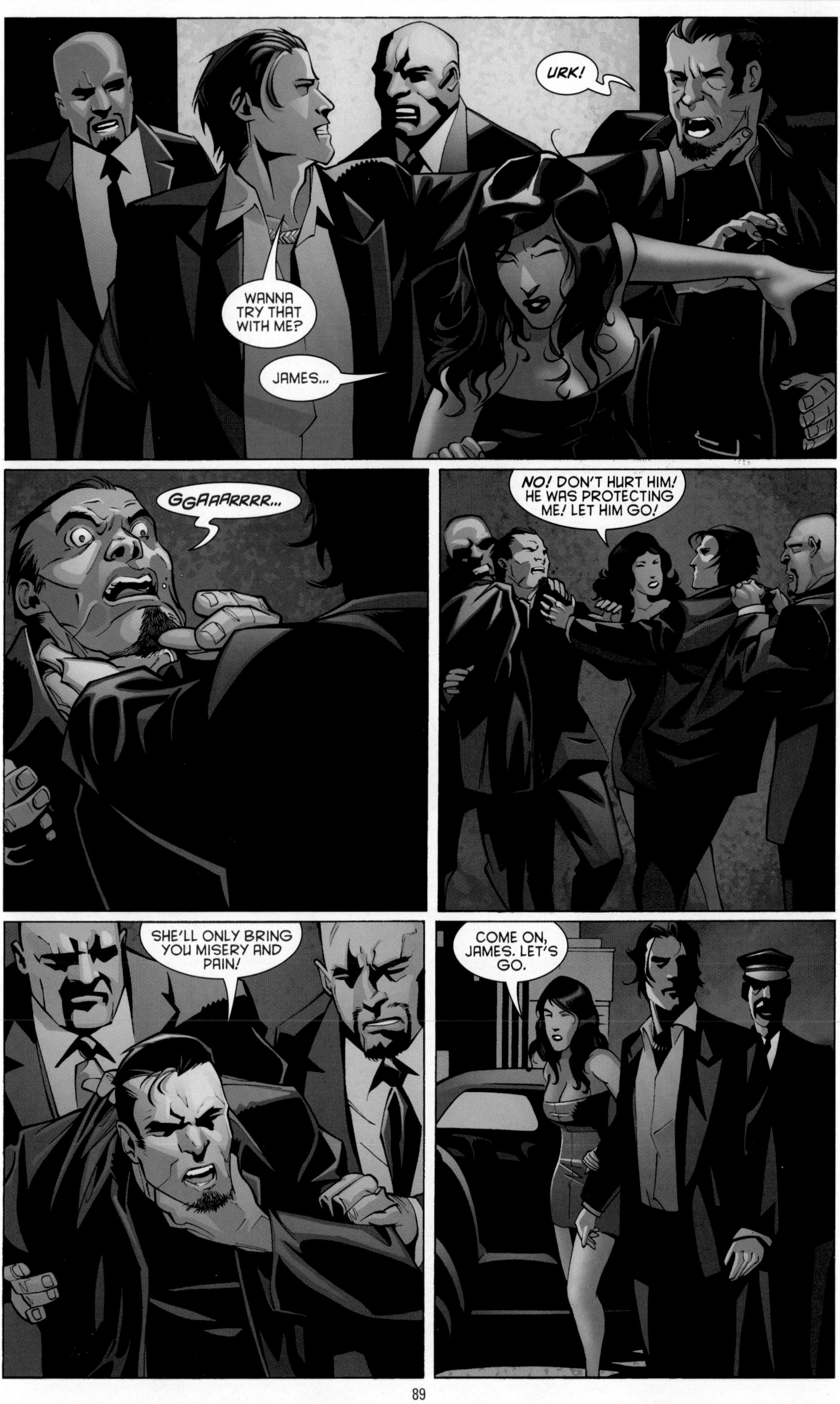
URK!
WANNA TRY THAT WITH ME?
JAMES...
GGAAARRRR...
NO! DON'T HURT HIM! HE WAS PROTECTING ME! LET HIM GO!
SHE'LL ONLY BRING YOU MISERY AND PAIN!
COME ON, JAMES. LET'S GO.

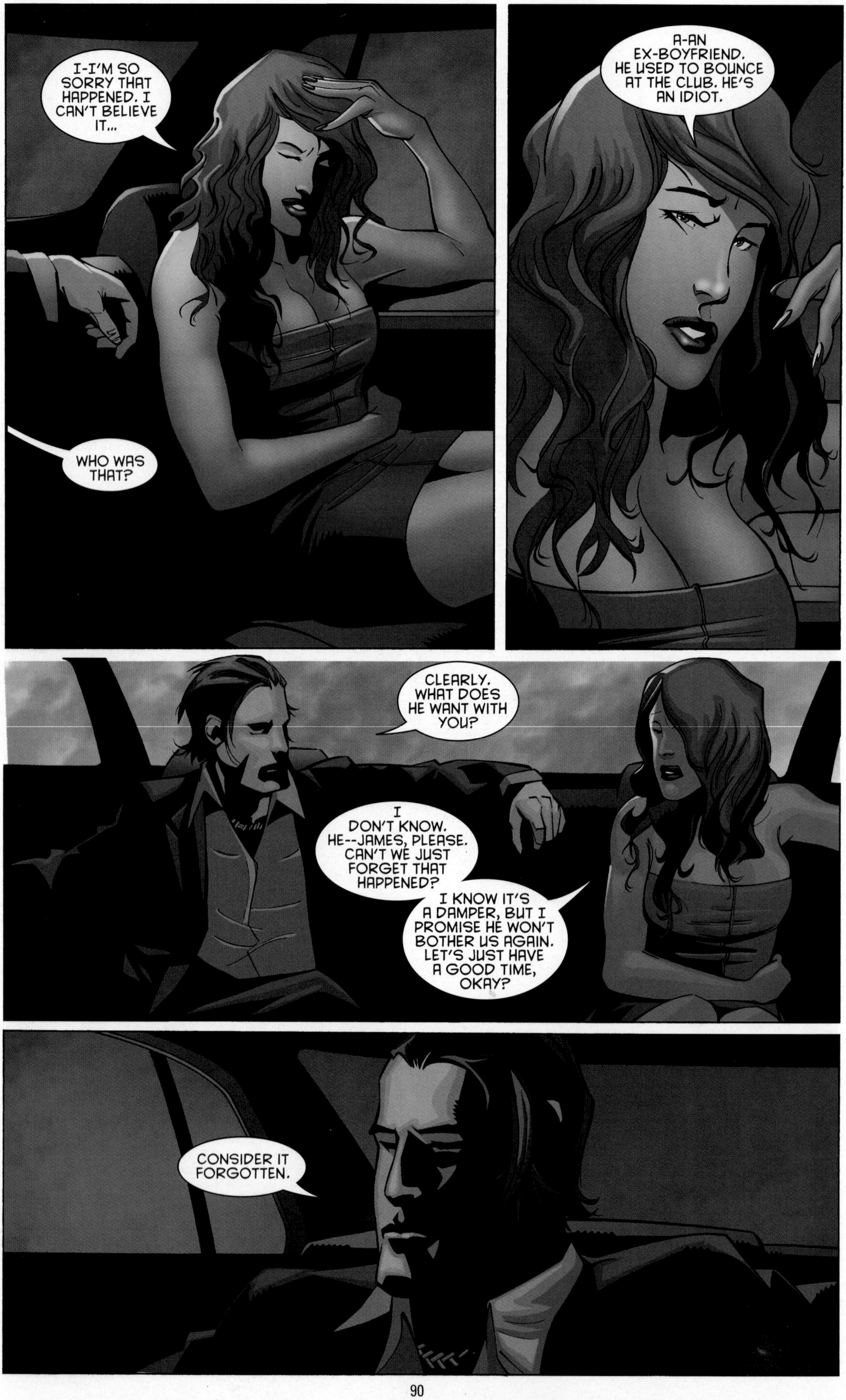
I-I'M SO SORRY THAT HAPPENED. I CAN'T BELIEVE IT...
WHO WAS THAT?
A-AN EX-BOYFRIEND. HE USED TO BOUNCE AT THE CLUB. HE'S AN IDIOT.
CLEARLY. WHAT DOES HE WANT WITH YOU?
I DON'T KNOW. HE--JAMES, PLEASE. CAN'T WE JUST FORGET THAT HAPPENED?
I KNOW IT'S A DAMPER, BUT I PROMISE HE WON'T BOTHER US AGAIN. LET'S JUST HAVE A GOOD TIME, OKAY?
CONSIDER IT FORGOTTEN.

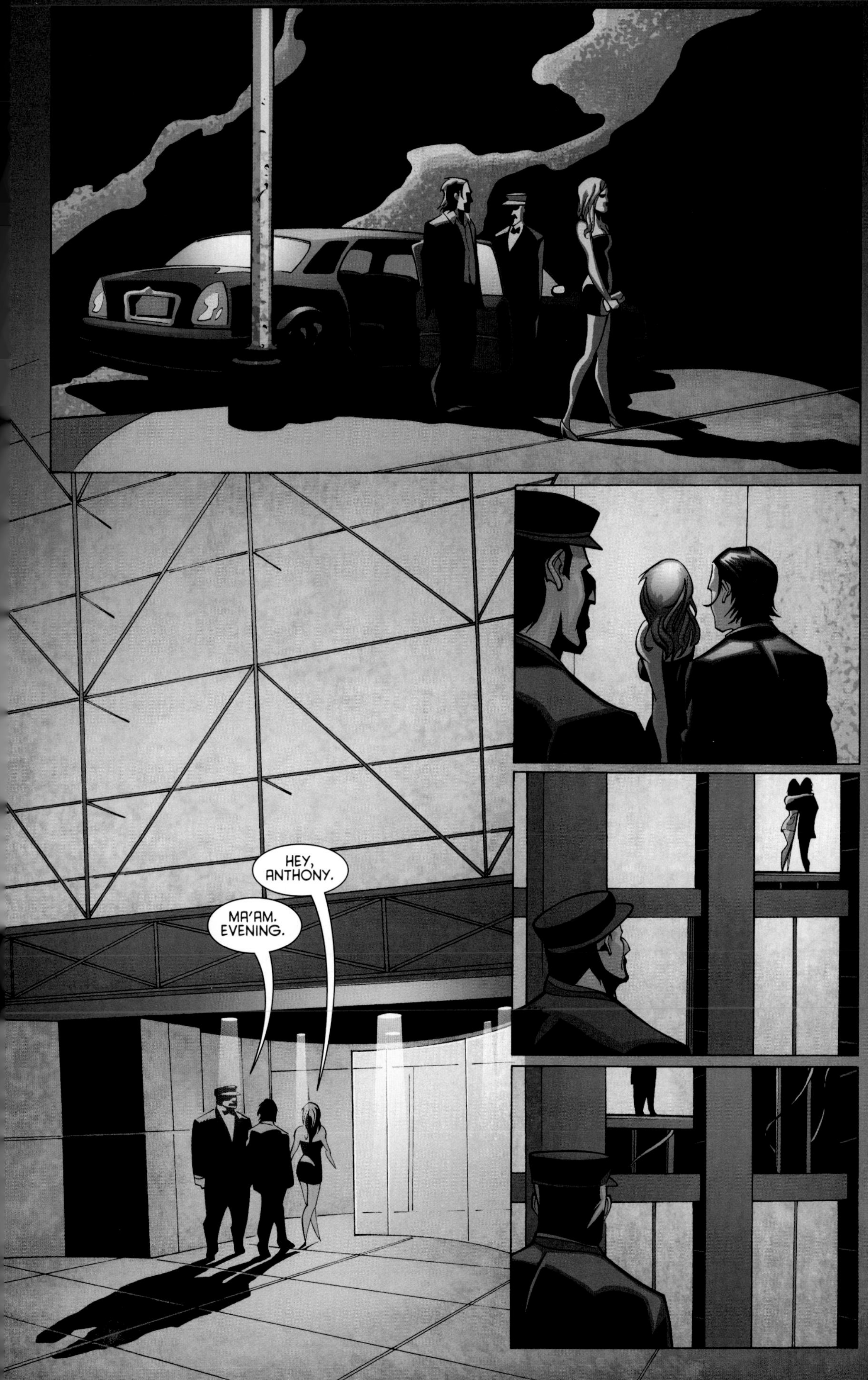
MA'AM. EVENING.
HEY, ANTHONY.

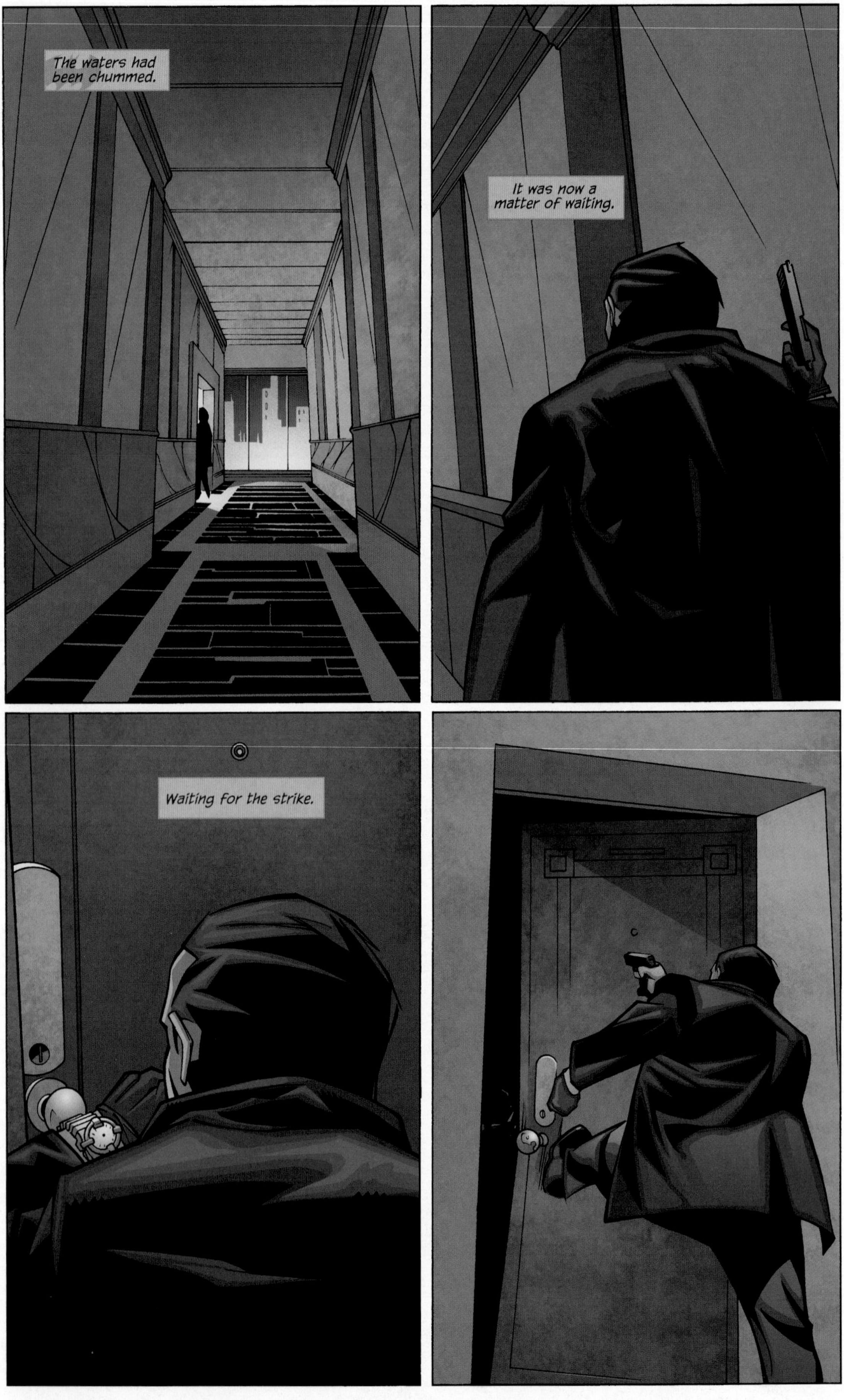
The waters had been chummed.
It was now a matter of waiting.
Waiting for the strike.

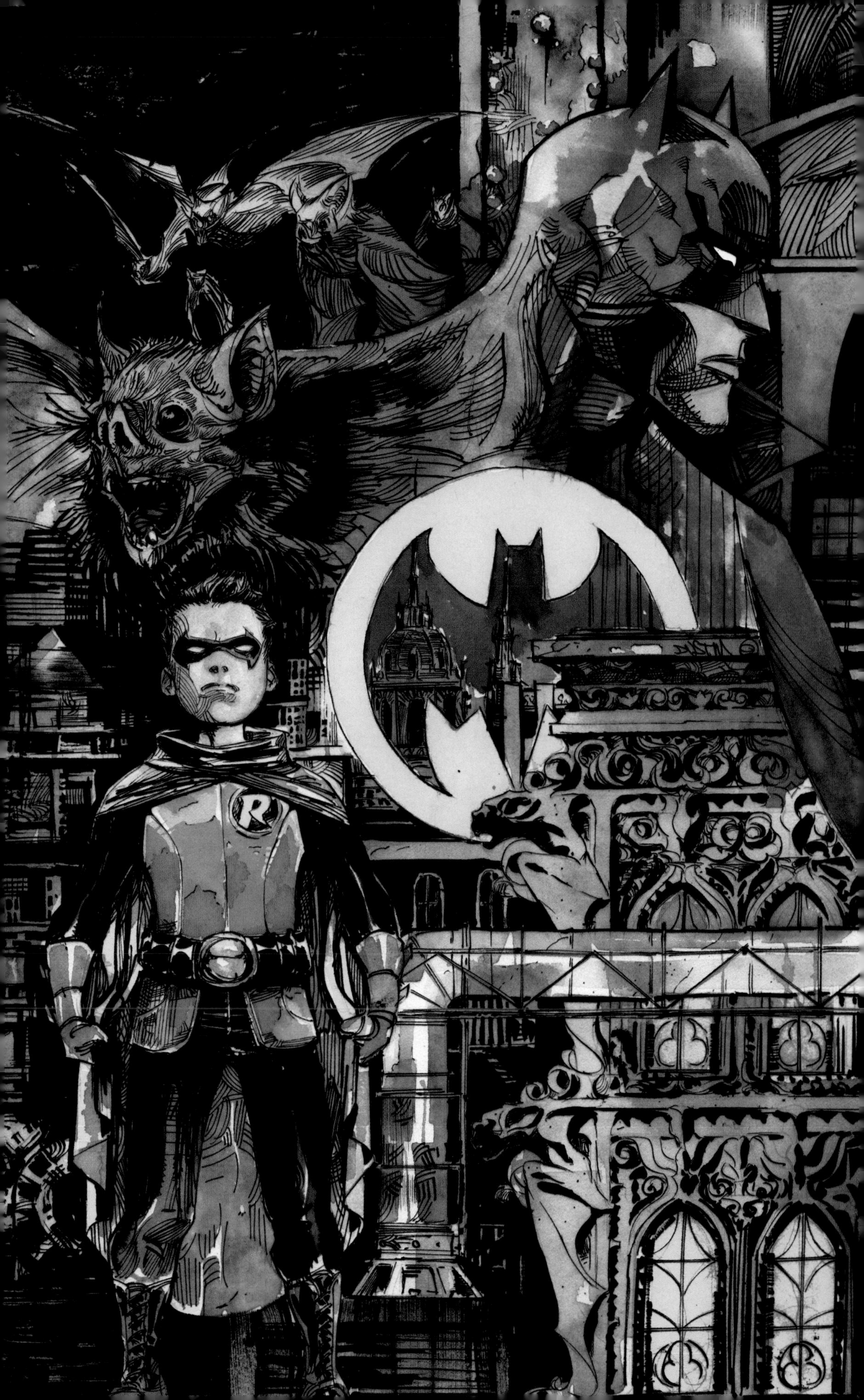

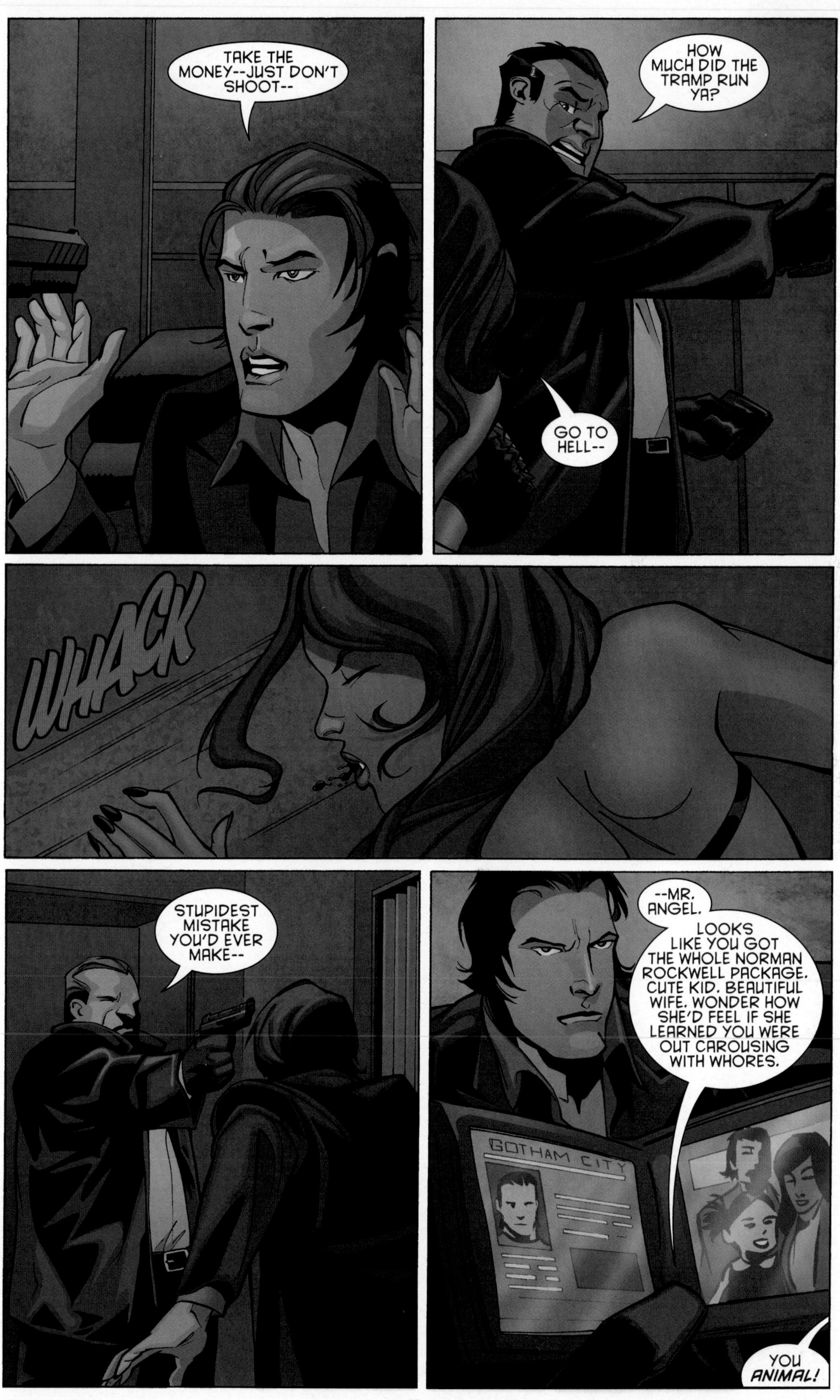
TAKE THE MONEY--JUST DON'T SHOOT--
HOW MUCH DID THE TRAMP RUN YA?
GO TO HELL--
WHACK
STUPIDEST MISTAKE YOU'D EVER MAKE--
--MR. ANGEL.
LOOKS LIKE YOU GOT THE WHOLE NORMAN ROCKWELL PACKAGE. CUTE KID. BEAUTIFUL WIFE. WONDER HOW SHE'D FEEL IF SHE LEARNED YOU WERE OUT CAROUSING WITH WHORES.
GOTHAM CITY
YOU *ANIMAL!*

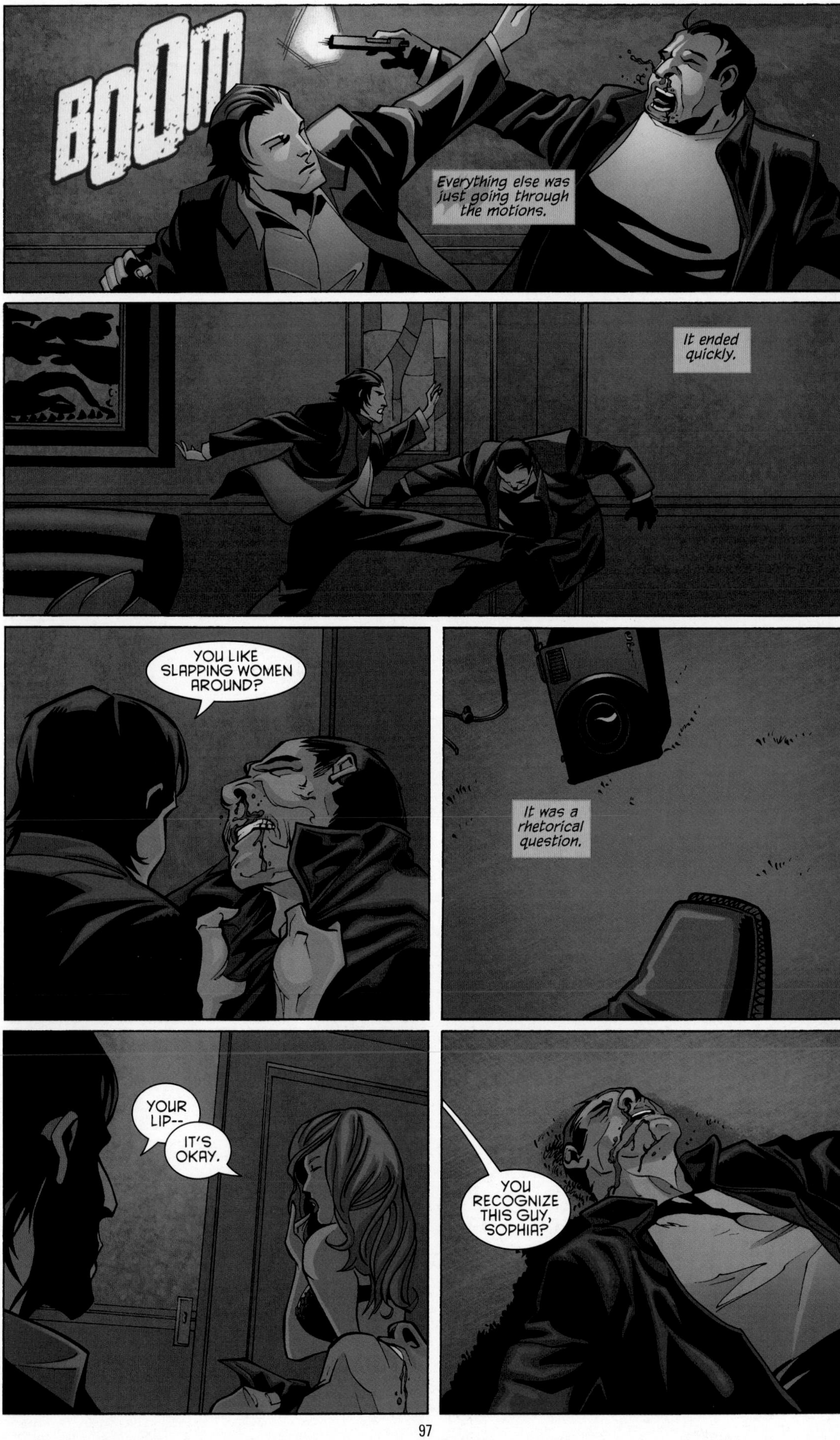
BOOM
Everything else was just going through the motions.
It ended quickly.
YOU LIKE SLAPPING WOMEN AROUND?
It was a rhetorical question.
YOUR LIP--
IT'S OKAY.
YOU RECOGNIZE THIS GUY, SOPHIA?

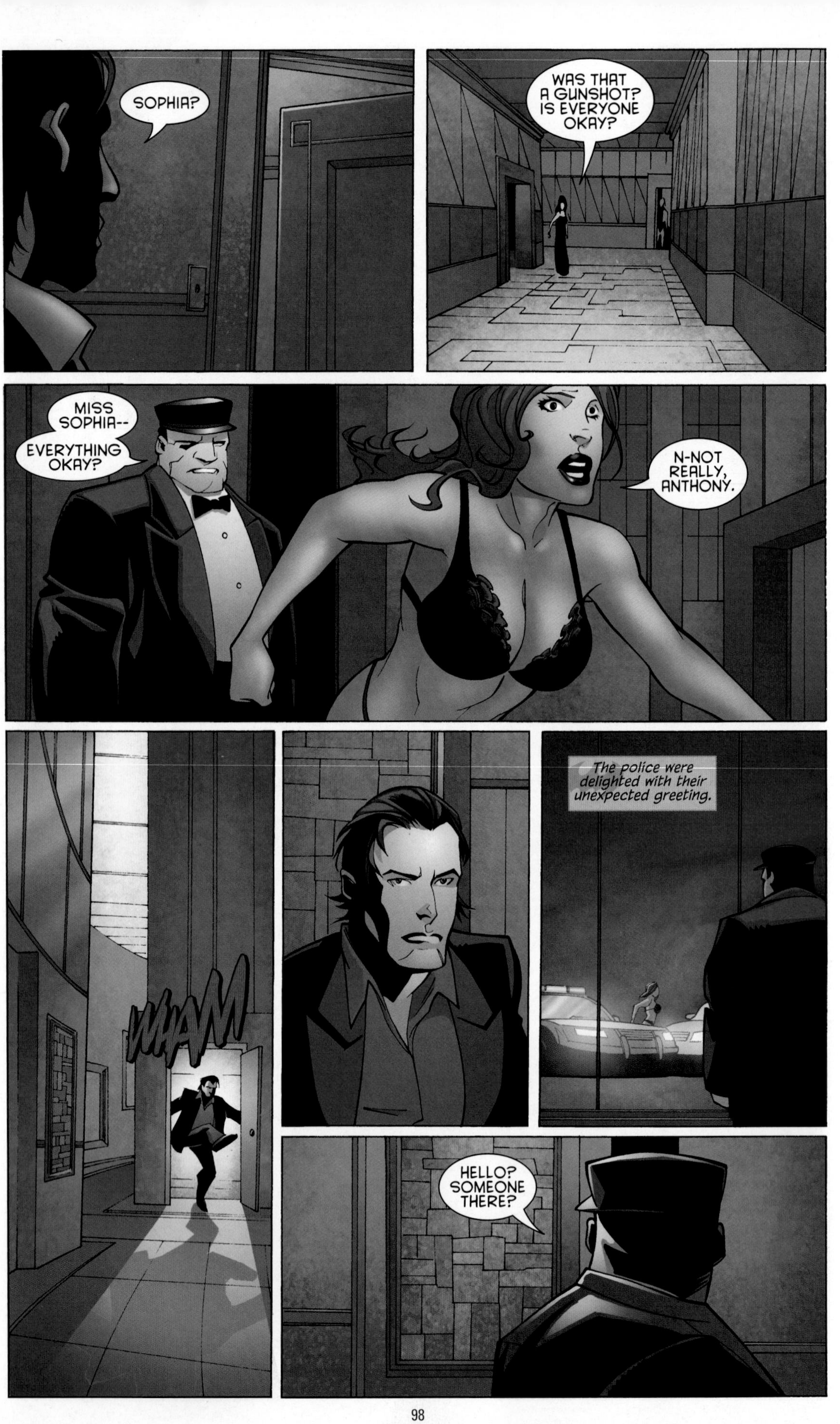
SOPHIA?
WAS THAT A GUNSHOT? IS EVERYONE OKAY?
MISS SOPHIA-- EVERYTHING OKAY?
N-NOT REALLY, ANTHONY.
WHAM
The police were delighted with their unexpected greeting.
HELLO? SOMEONE THERE?

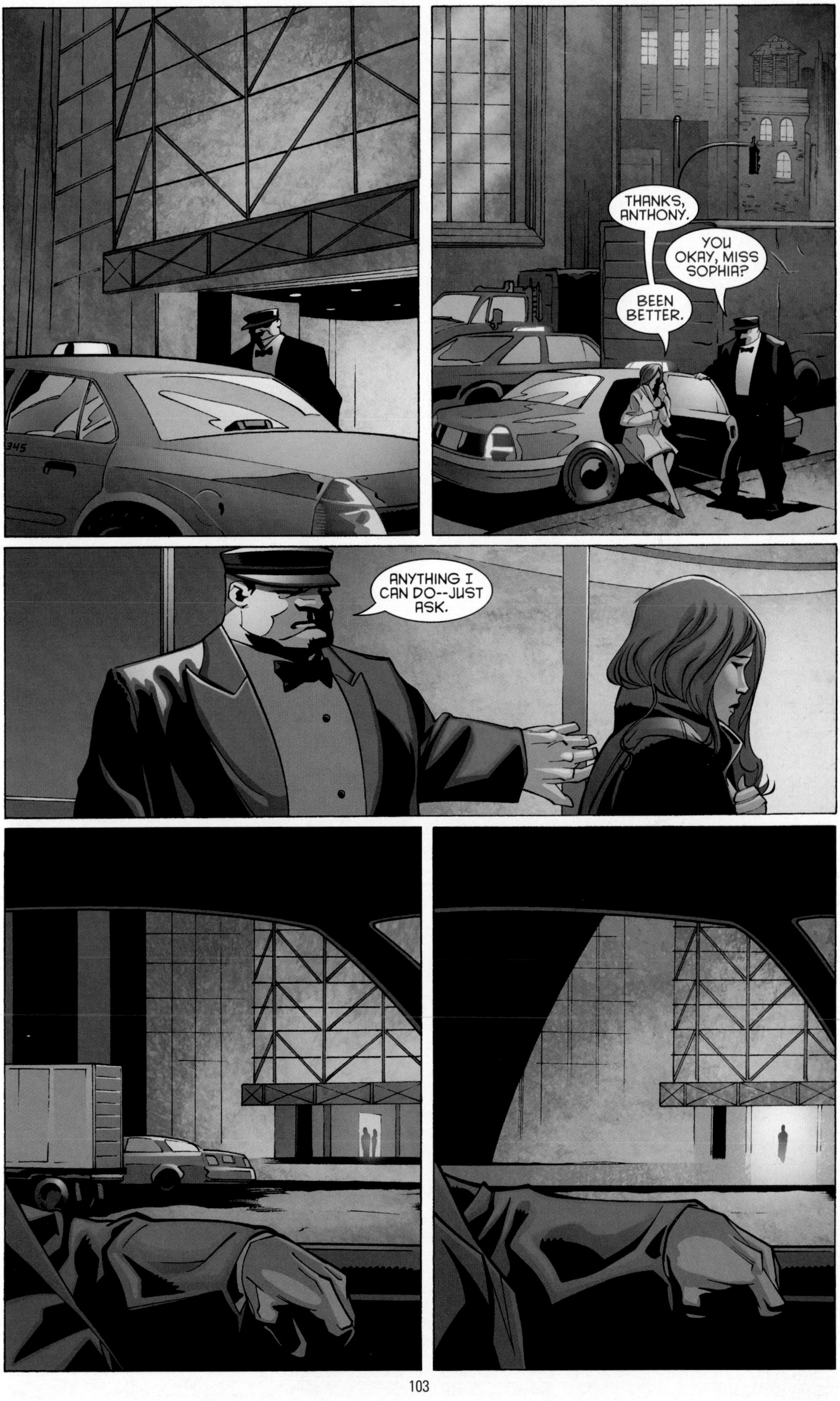
THANKS, ANTHONY.
YOU OKAY, MISS SOPHIA?
BEEN BETTER.
ANYTHING I CAN DO--JUST ASK.

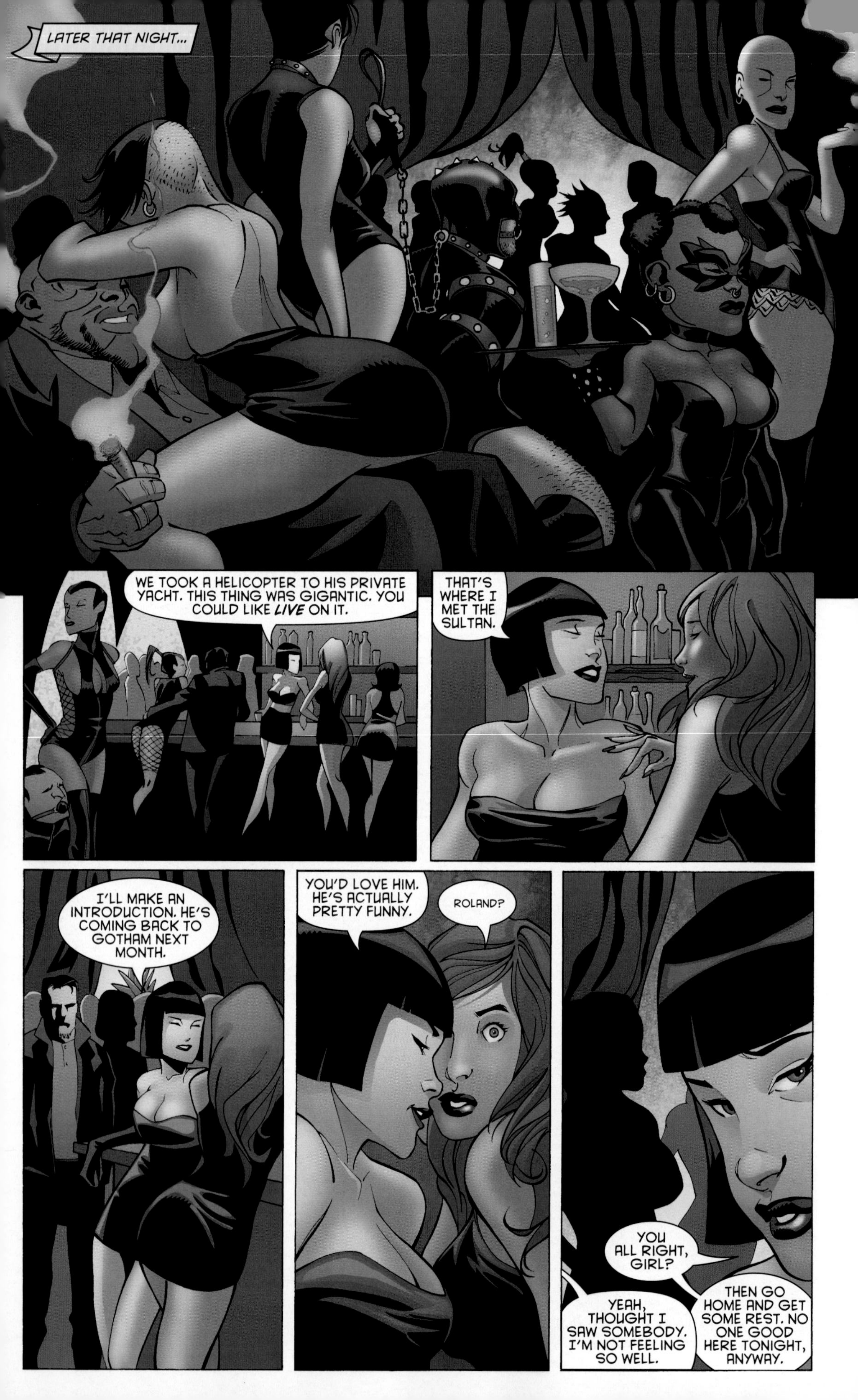
LATER THAT NIGHT...
WE TOOK A HELICOPTER TO HIS PRIVATE YACHT. THIS THING WAS GIGANTIC. YOU COULD LIKE *LIVE* ON IT.
THAT'S WHERE I MET THE SULTAN.
I'LL MAKE AN INTRODUCTION. HE'S COMING BACK TO GOTHAM NEXT MONTH.
YOU'D LOVE HIM. HE'S ACTUALLY PRETTY FUNNY.
ROLAND?
YOU ALL RIGHT, GIRL?
YEAH, THOUGHT I SAW SOMEBODY. I'M NOT FEELING SO WELL.
THEN GO HOME AND GET SOME REST. NO ONE GOOD HERE TONIGHT, ANYWAY.

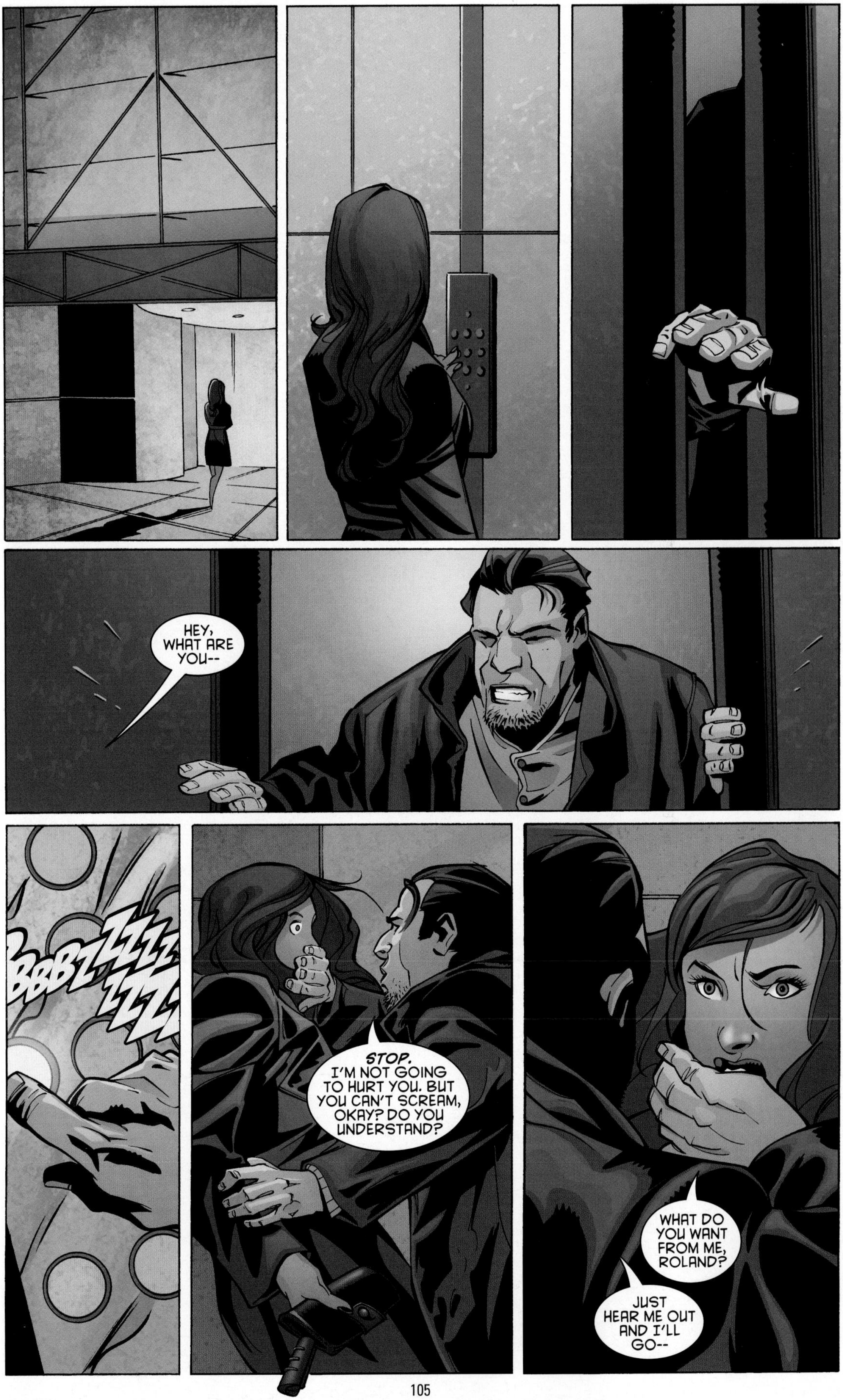
HEY, WHAT ARE YOU--
BBBZZZZZZ
STOP. I'M NOT GOING TO HURT YOU. BUT YOU CAN'T SCREAM, OKAY? DO YOU UNDERSTAND?
WHAT DO YOU WANT FROM ME, ROLAND?
JUST HEAR ME OUT AND I'LL GO--

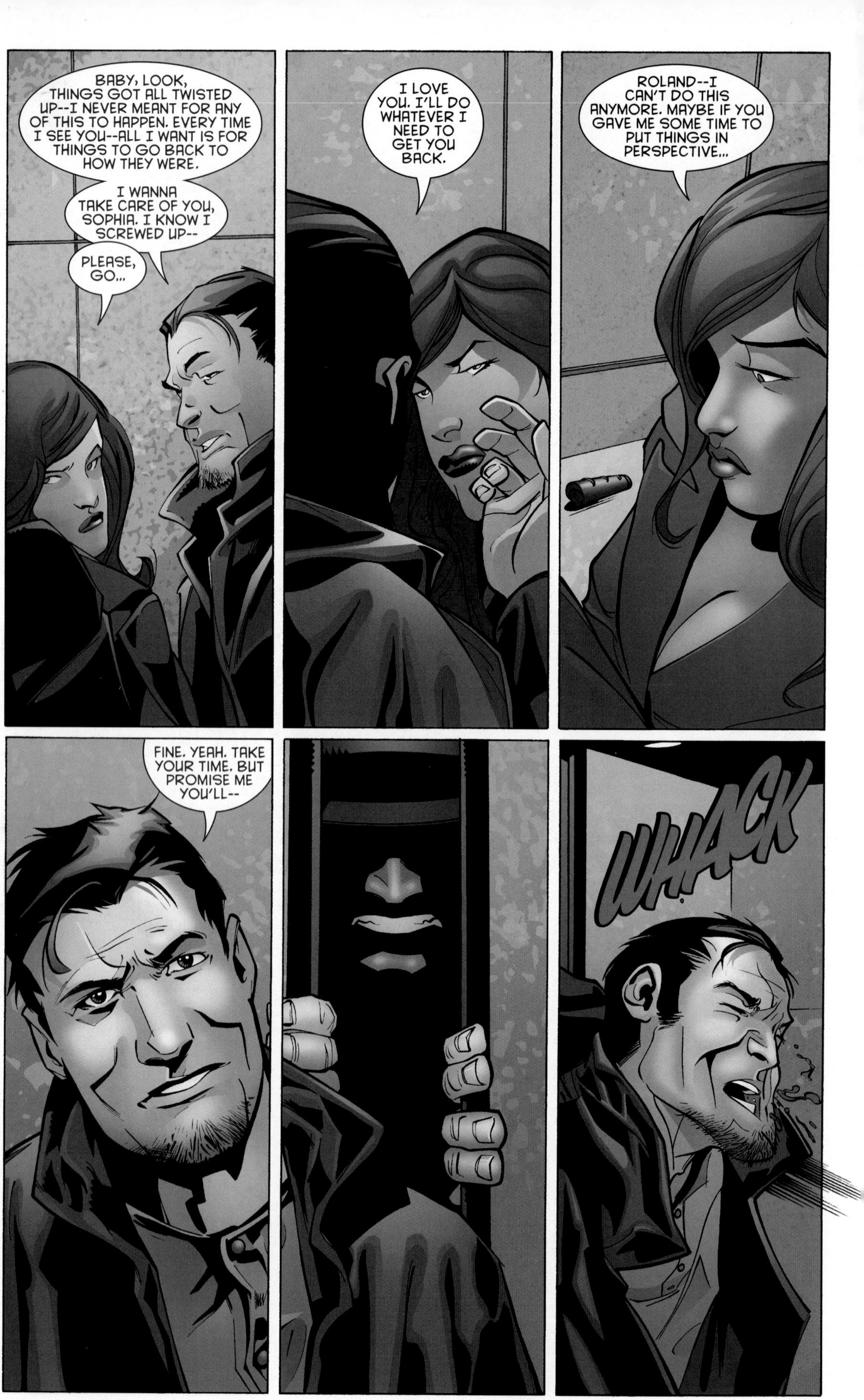
BABY, LOOK, THINGS GOT ALL TWISTED UP--I NEVER MEANT FOR ANY OF THIS TO HAPPEN. EVERY TIME I SEE YOU--ALL I WANT IS FOR THINGS TO GO BACK TO HOW THEY WERE.
I WANNA TAKE CARE OF YOU, SOPHIA. I KNOW I SCREWED UP--
PLEASE, GO...
I LOVE YOU. I'LL DO WHATEVER I NEED TO GET YOU BACK.
ROLAND--I CAN'T DO THIS ANYMORE. MAYBE IF YOU GAVE ME SOME TIME TO PUT THINGS IN PERSPECTIVE...
FINE. YEAH. TAKE YOUR TIME. BUT PROMISE ME YOU'LL--
WHACK

WHY YOU KEEP SAYING THAT?

YOU WERE SPOTTED AT THE CLUB THE NIGHT OF EACH MURDER.

I'M TELLING YOU THE TRUTH.

SO YOU SAY.

YOU WANNA PLAY THESE GAMES--YOU'RE GONNA COME OUT ON THE BOTTOM.

THIS IS CRAP, MAN-- YOU CAN'T DO THIS. THIS AIN'T RIGHT, WHAT HAPPENED TO MY RIGHTS--

YOU LOST THEM WHEN YOU STARTED KILLING PEOPLE.

YOU COULDN'T STAND SEEING SOPHIA WITH OTHER MEN. YOU STARTED UP WITH EACH OF THEM--

GOT ANY HARD EVIDENCE-- ANY OF MY BLOOD? I MAY HAVE SLAPPED HER BUT I DIDN'T KILL ANYONE, FREAK.

YOU KILLED THOSE MEN.

WHAPP

THAT'LL BE ENOUGH, BATMAN.

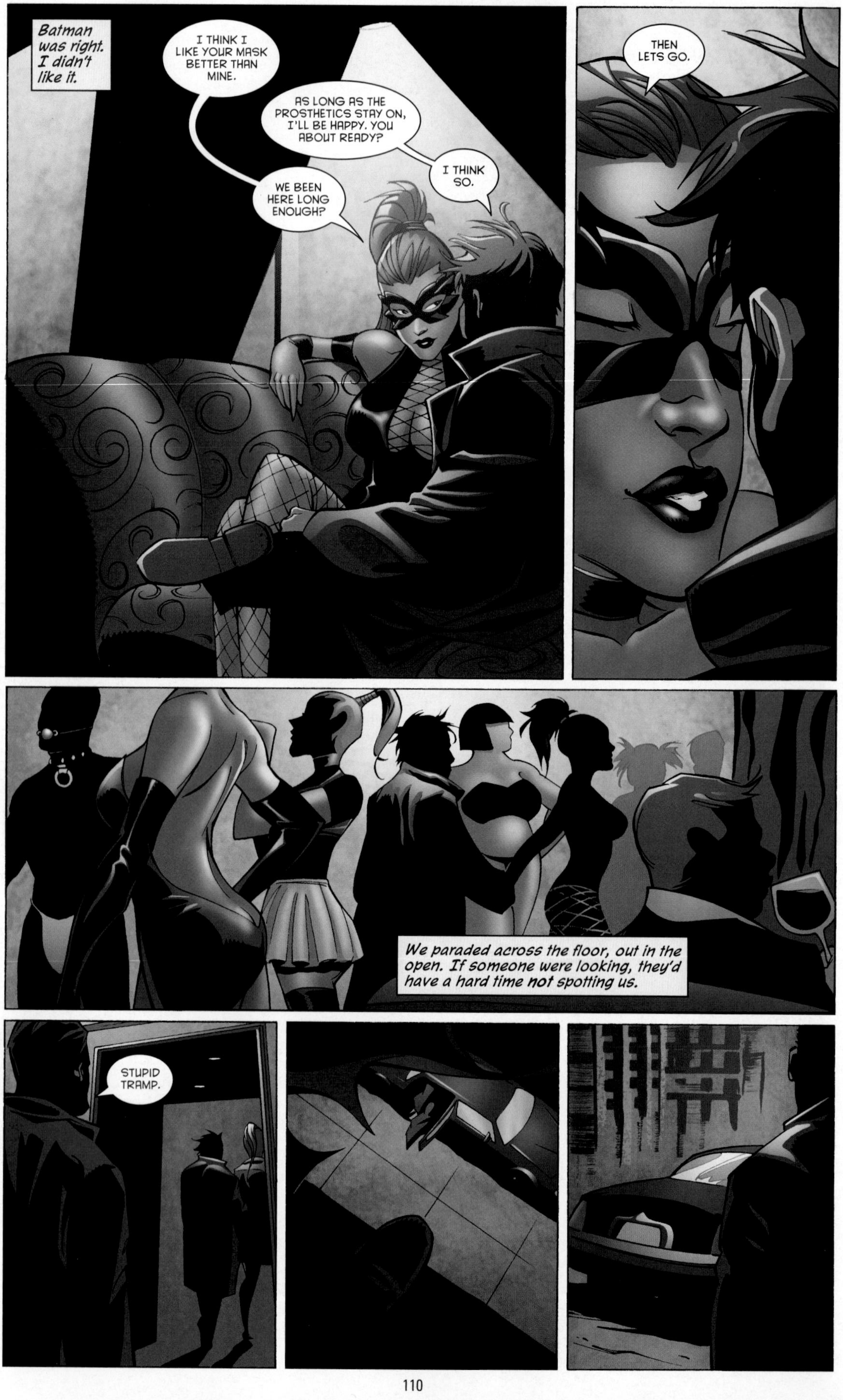
Batman was right. I didn't like it.
I THINK I LIKE YOUR MASK BETTER THAN MINE.
AS LONG AS THE PROSTHETICS STAY ON, I'LL BE HAPPY. YOU ABOUT READY?
I THINK SO.
WE BEEN HERE LONG ENOUGH?
THEN LETS GO.
We paraded across the floor, out in the open. If someone were looking, they'd have a hard time not spotting us.
STUPID TRAMP.

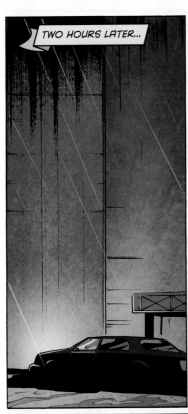

TWO HOURS LATER...

YOU DIDN'T
ANSWER MY
QUESTION.

DON'T
COME ANY
CLOSER.

LET ME
SEE YOUR
HANDS.

BAM

HAPPY
TO...

...THEY'LL BE
HOLDING MY
KNIFE...

AHHHH!

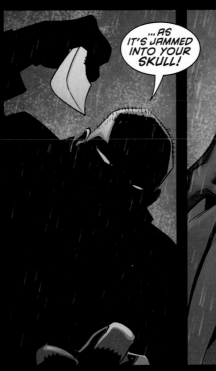

...AS
IT'S JAMMED
INTO YOUR
SKULL!

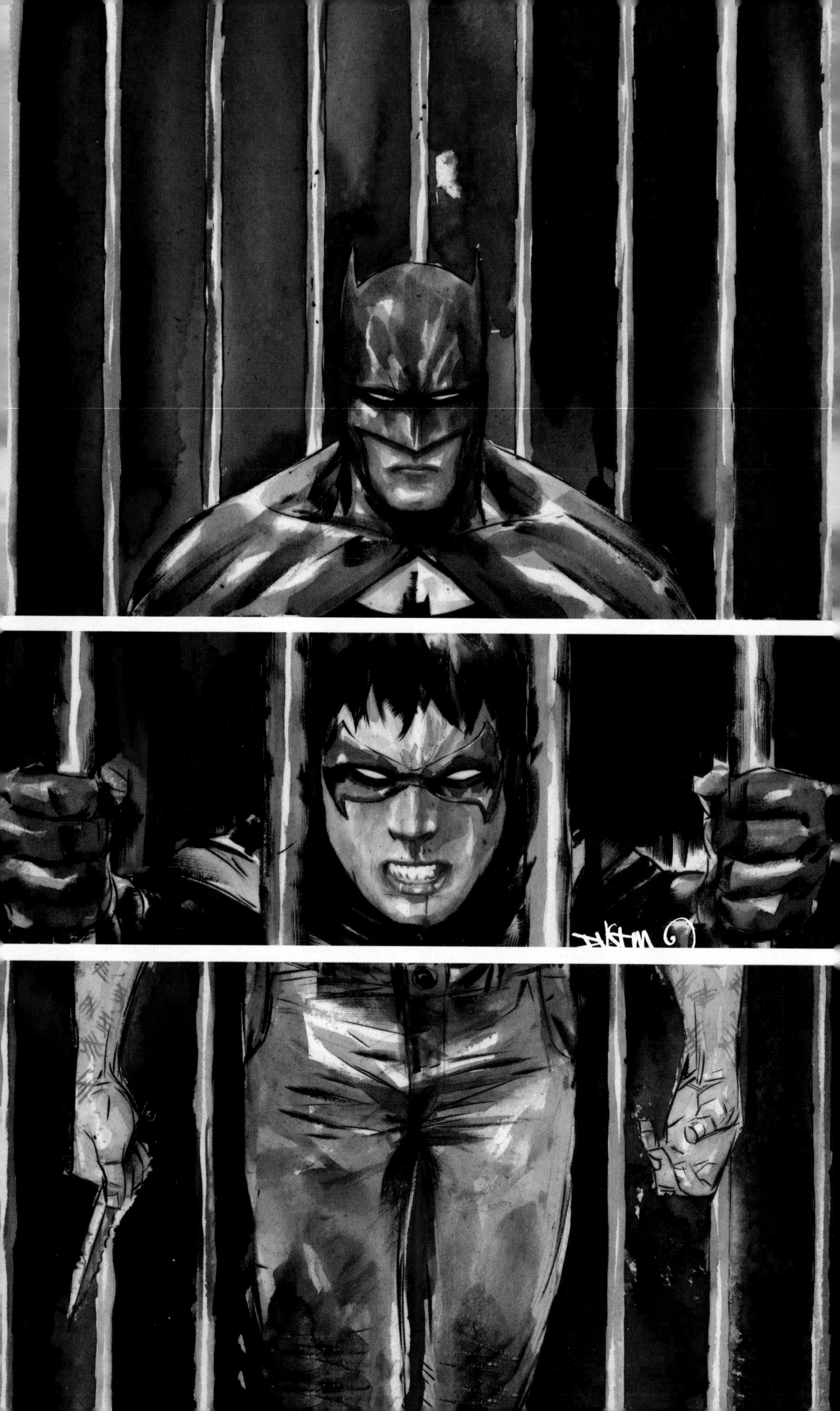

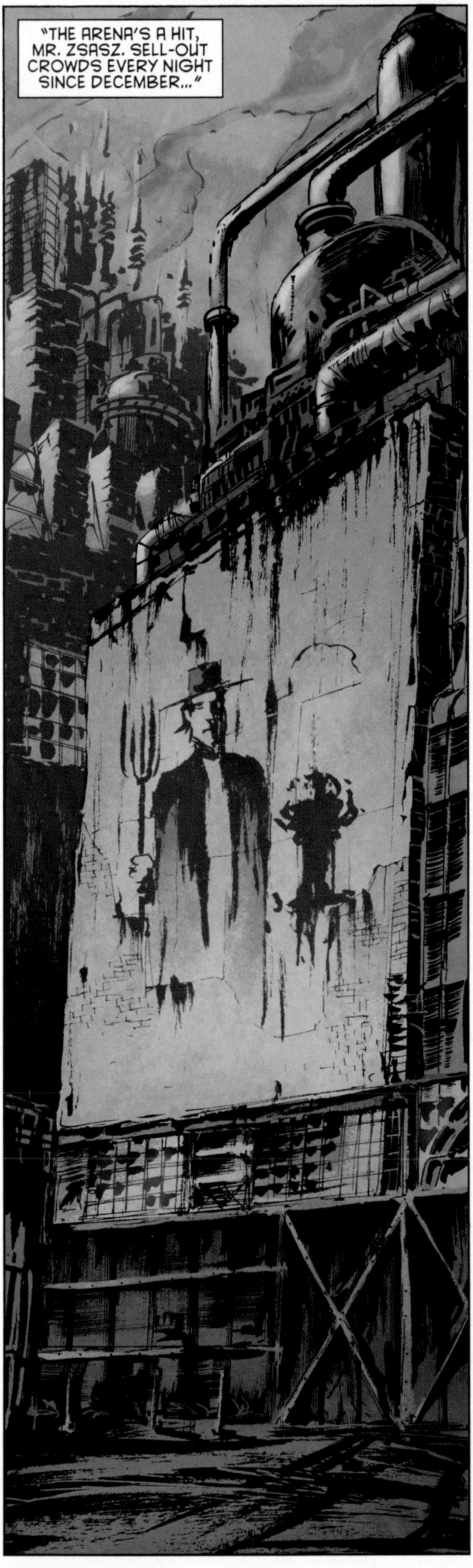
"THE ARENA'S A HIT, MR. ZSASZ. SELL-OUT CROWDS EVERY NIGHT SINCE DECEMBER..."

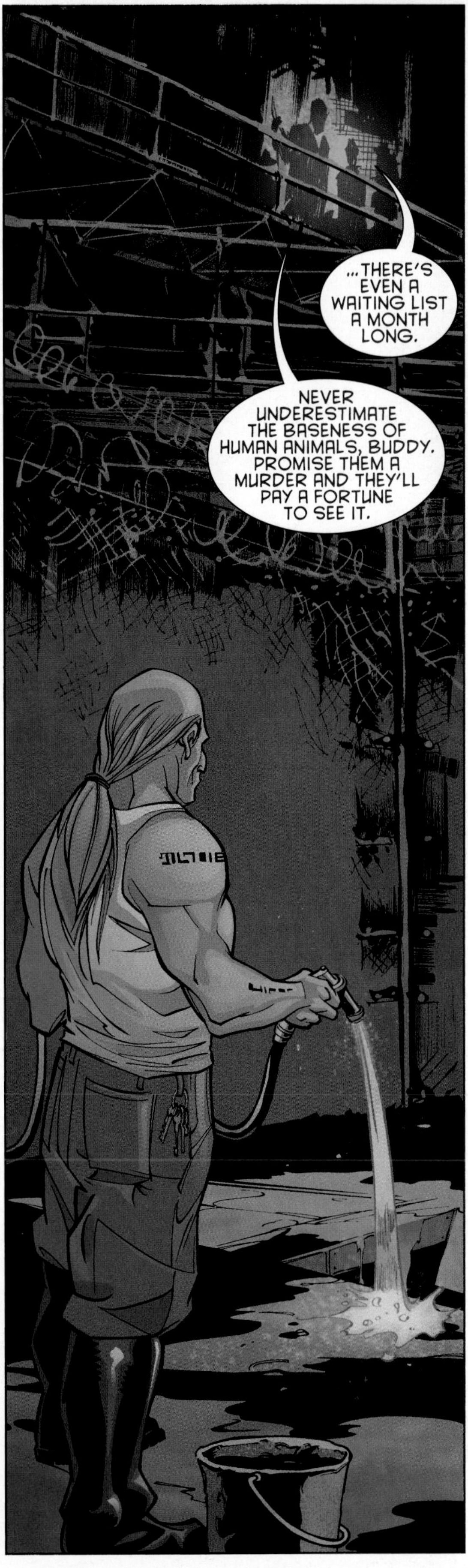
...THERE'S EVEN A WAITING LIST A MONTH LONG.
NEVER UNDERESTIMATE THE BASENESS OF HUMAN ANIMALS, BUDDY. PROMISE THEM A MURDER AND THEY'LL PAY A FORTUNE TO SEE IT.

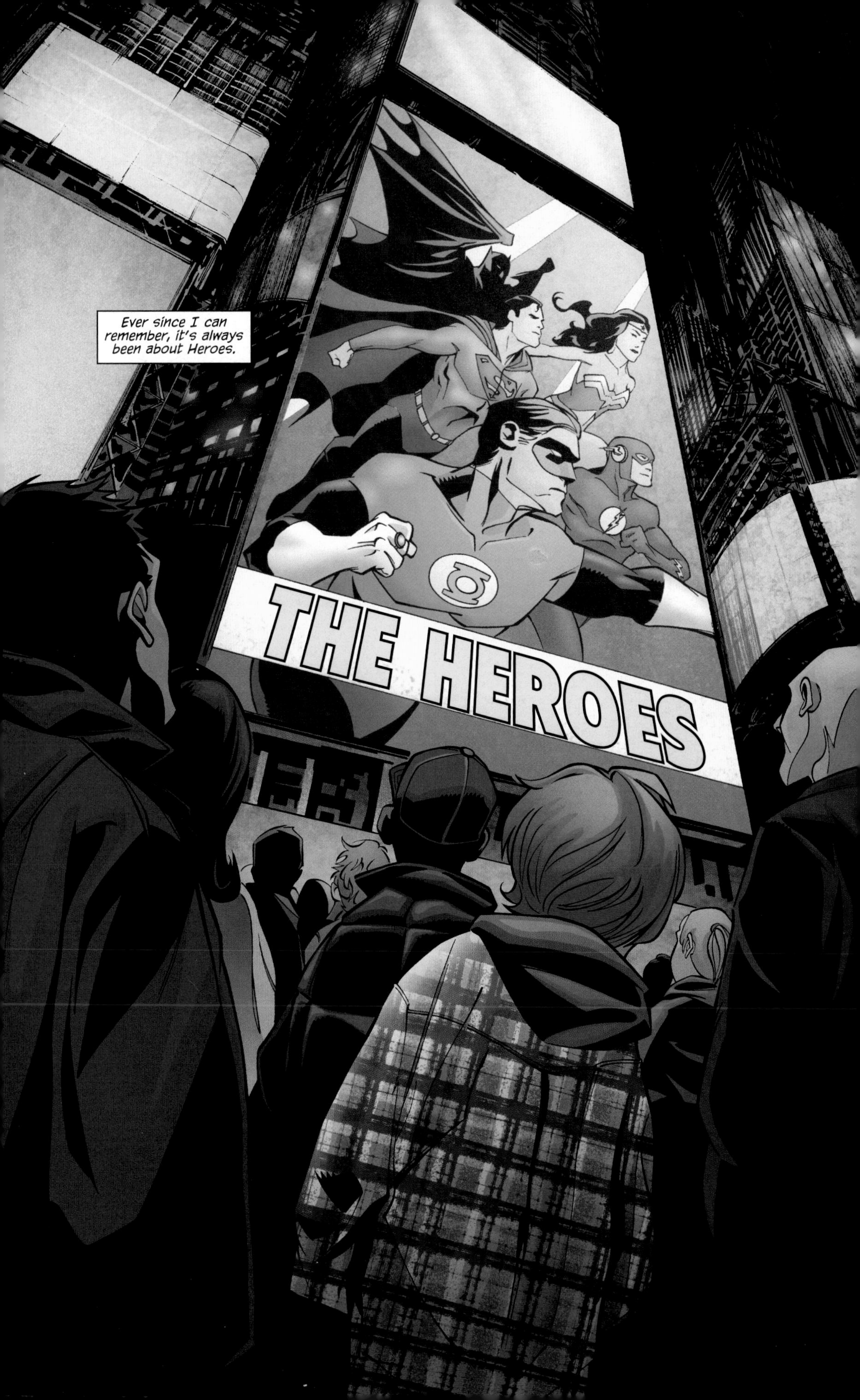
Ever since I can remember, it's always been about Heroes.
THE HEROES

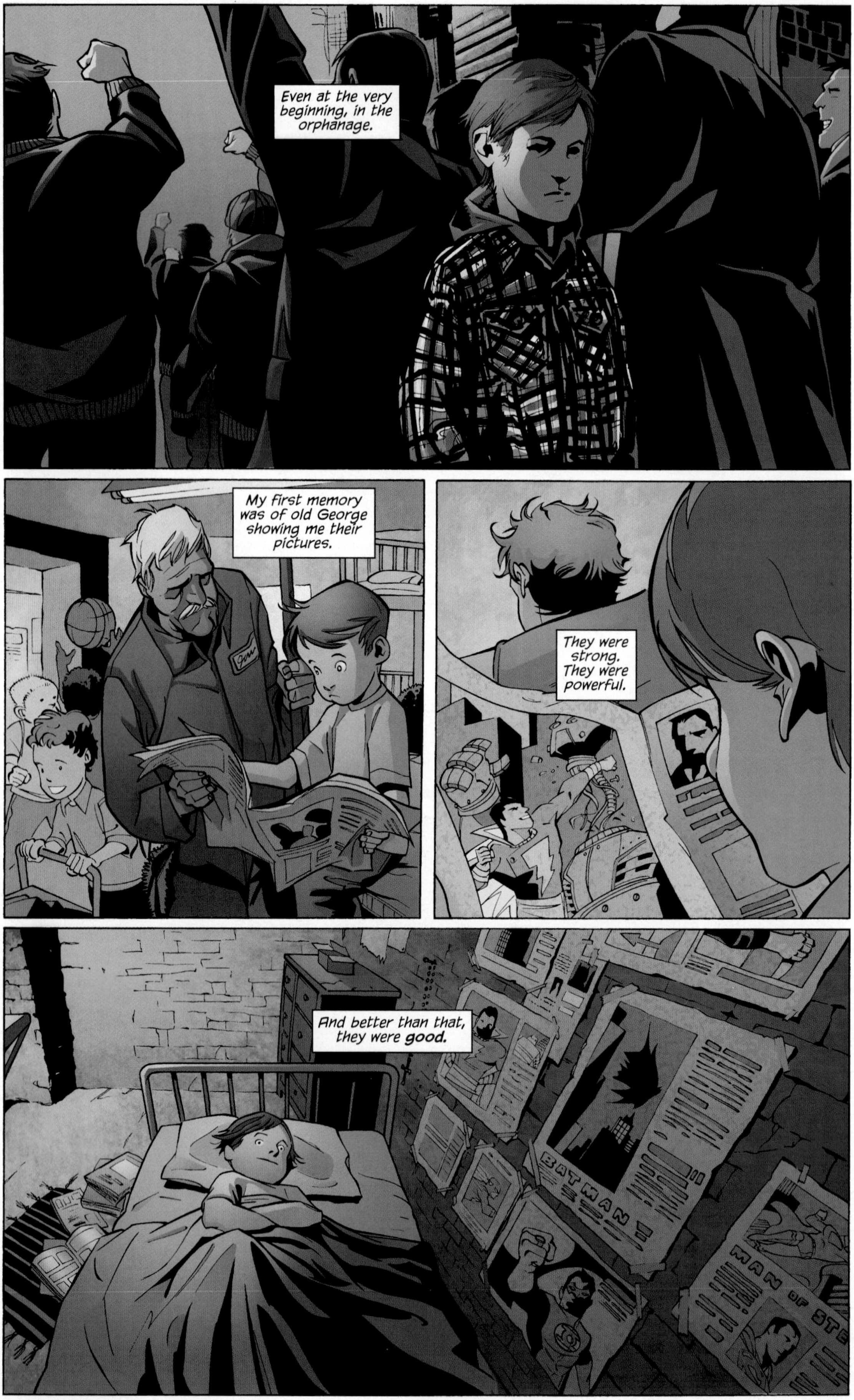
Even at the very beginning, in the orphanage.
My first memory was of old George showing me their pictures.
They were strong. They were powerful.
And better than that, they were **good.**
BATMAN!

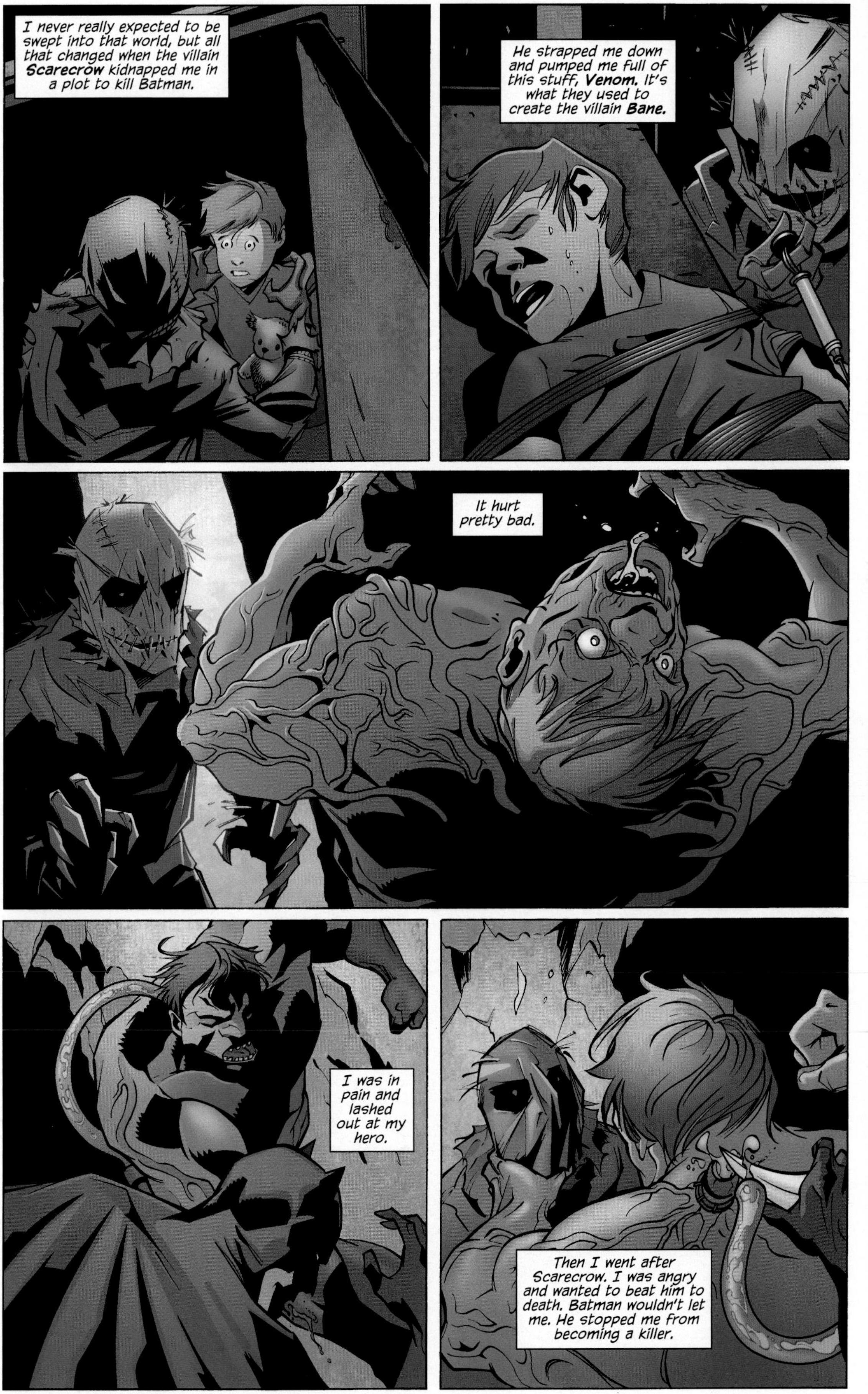
I never really expected to be swept into that world, but all that changed when the villain Scarecrow kidnapped me in a plot to kill Batman.
He strapped me down and pumped me full of this stuff, Venom. It's what they used to create the villain Bane.
It hurt pretty bad.
I was in pain and lashed out at my hero.
Then I went after Scarecrow. I was angry and wanted to beat him to death. Batman wouldn't let me. He stopped me from becoming a killer.

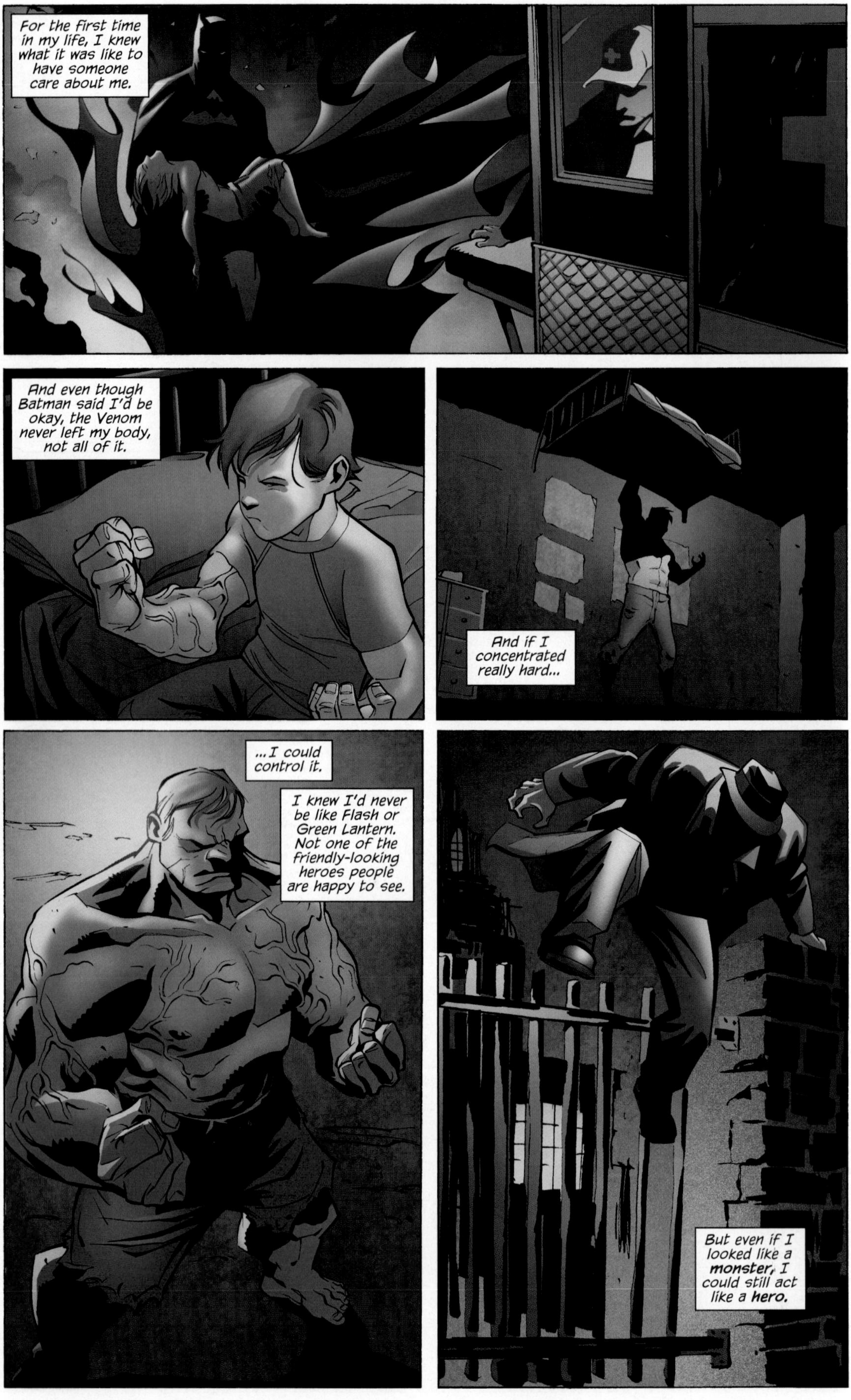

For the first time in my life, I knew what it was like to have someone care about me.
And even though Batman said I'd be okay, the Venom never left my body, not all of it.
And if I concentrated really hard...
...I could control it.
I knew I'd never be like Flash or Green Lantern. Not one of the friendly-looking heroes people are happy to see.
But even if I looked like a **monster**, I could still act like a **hero.**

I started with some thugs who used to prey on us orphans. They knew we didn't have any money, they just beat us up for the fun of it.

I had some laughs myself that night.

Sister Agnes taught me stealing is a *sin*.

And even though I knew I shouldn't, I took the gangsters' jewelry. I needed something.

I cashed it in at a pawn shop and took the money to someone I'd heard about, someone I wasn't sure even existed. After a few days, I finally found her.

I'M LOOKING FOR JONESY. I WANT TO BUY SOMETHING.

THIS AIN'T WAL-MART. GET LOST.

CRUNNCH

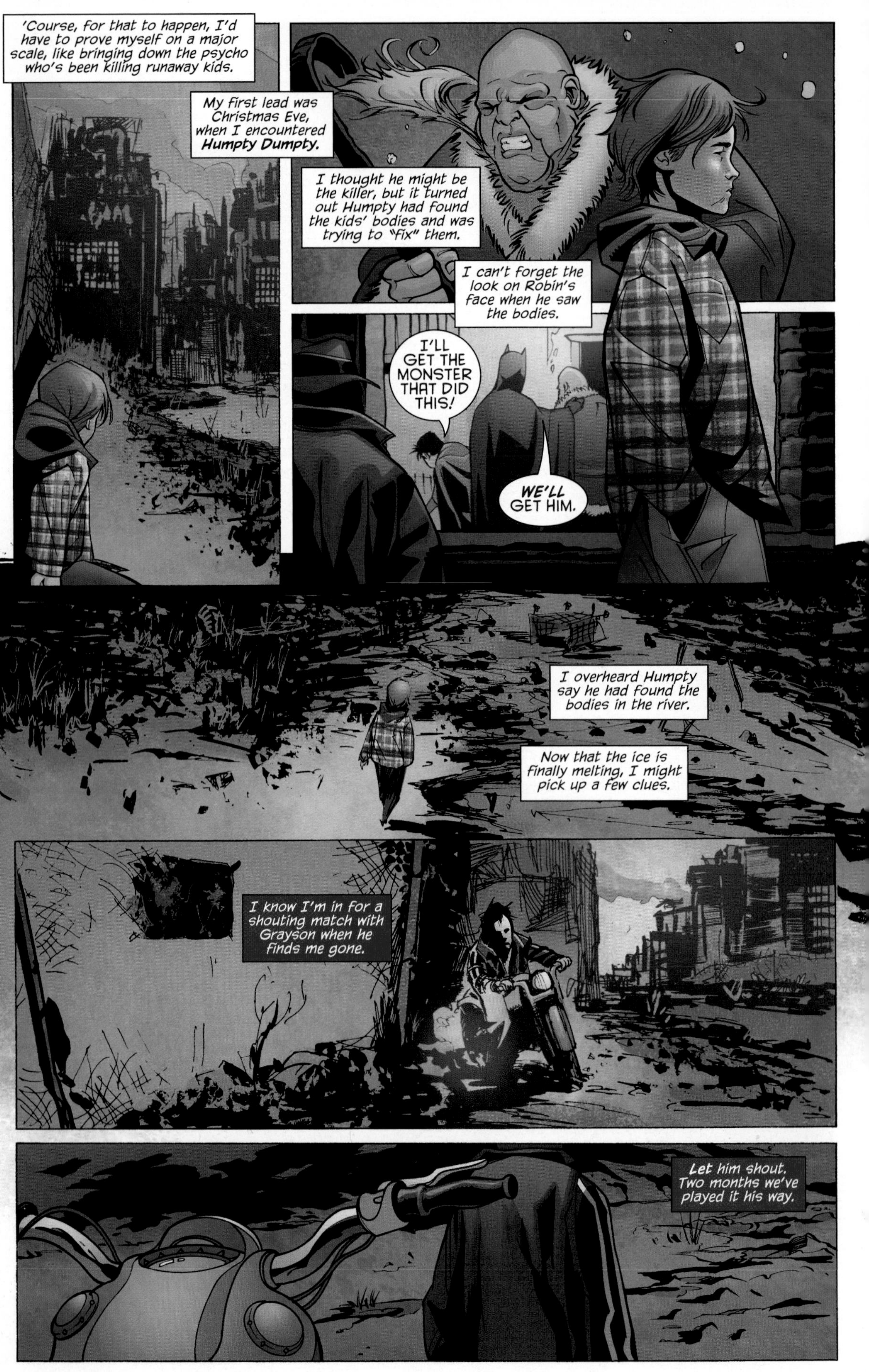
'Course, for that to happen, I'd have to prove myself on a major scale, like bringing down the psycho who's been killing runaway kids.
My first lead was Christmas Eve, when I encountered **Humpty Dumpty.**
I thought he might be the killer, but it turned out Humpty had found the kids' bodies and was trying to "fix" them.
I can't forget the look on Robin's face when he saw the bodies.
I'LL GET THE MONSTER THAT DID THIS!
WE'LL GET HIM.
I overheard Humpty say he had found the bodies in the river.
Now that the ice is finally melting, I might pick up a few clues.
I know I'm in for a shouting match with Grayson when he finds me gone.
Let him shout. Two months we've played it his way.

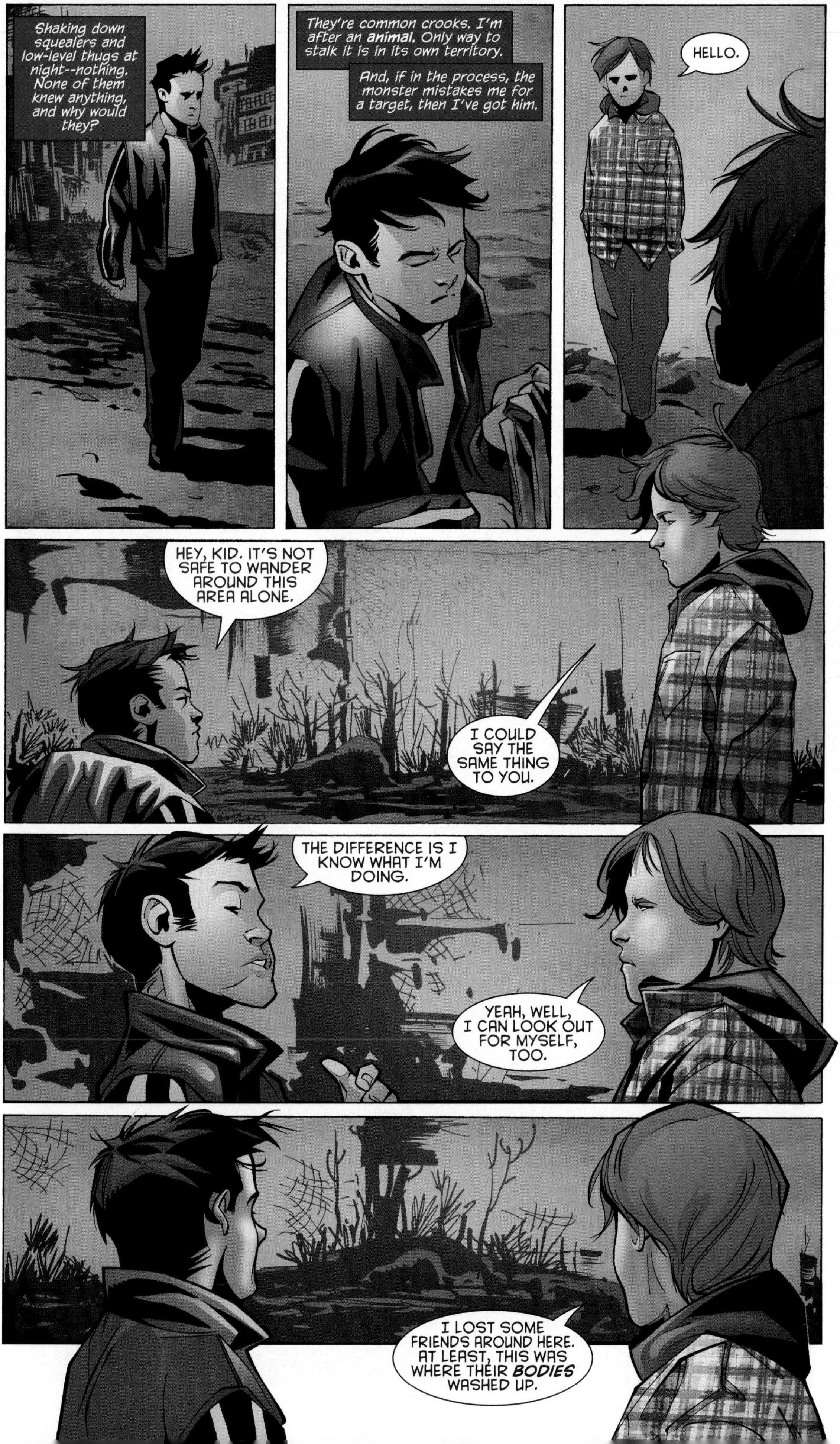
Shaking down squealers and low-level thugs at night--nothing. None of them knew anything, and why would they?
They're common crooks. I'm after an **animal.** Only way to stalk it is in its own territory.
And, if in the process, the monster mistakes me for a target, then I've got him.
HELLO.
HEY, KID. IT'S NOT SAFE TO WANDER AROUND THIS AREA ALONE.
I COULD SAY THE SAME THING TO YOU.
THE DIFFERENCE IS I KNOW WHAT I'M DOING.
YEAH, WELL, I CAN LOOK OUT FOR MYSELF, TOO.
I LOST SOME FRIENDS AROUND HERE. AT LEAST, THIS WAS WHERE THEIR ***BODIES*** WASHED UP.

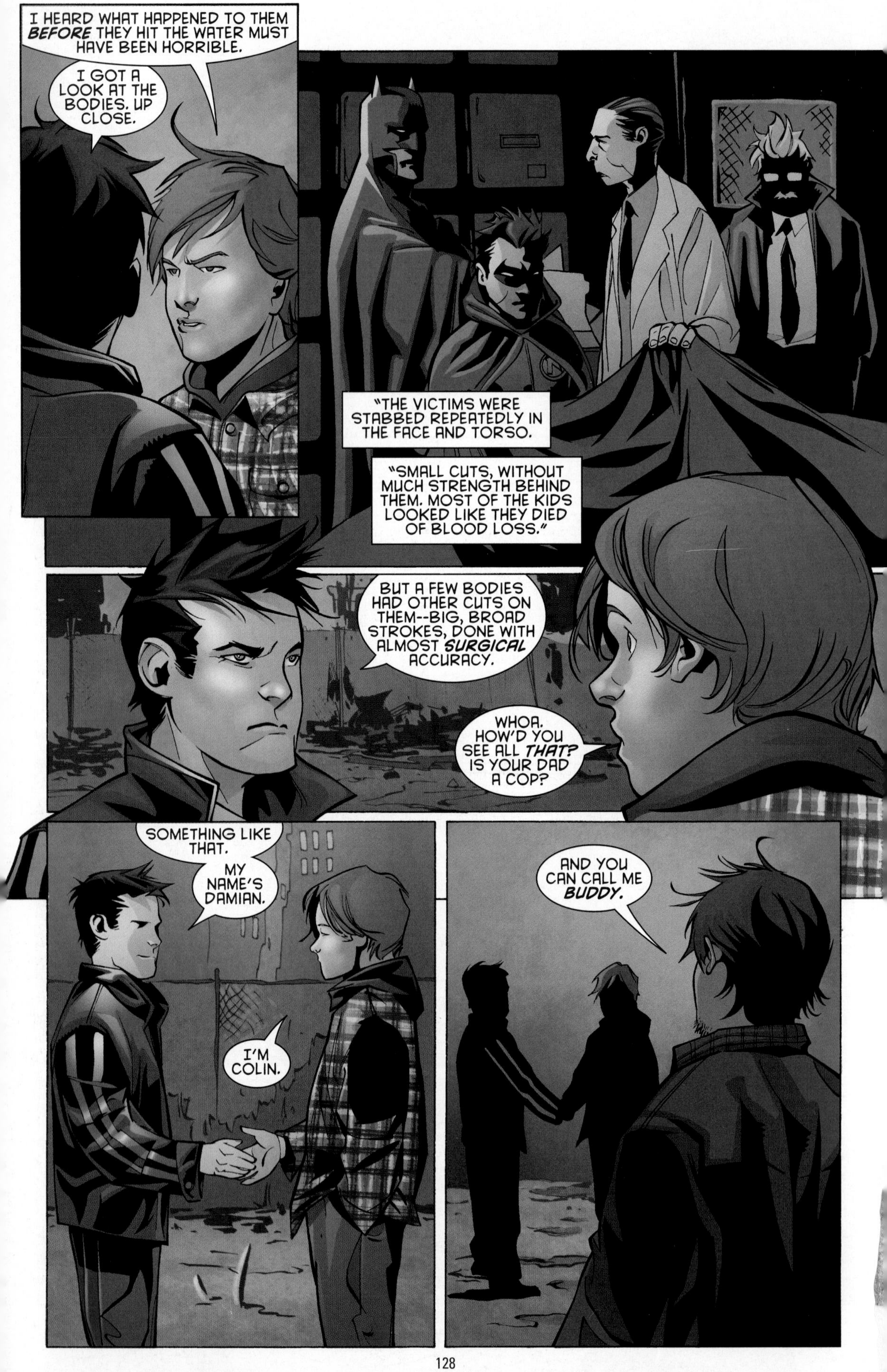

I HEARD WHAT HAPPENED TO THEM BEFORE THEY HIT THE WATER MUST HAVE BEEN HORRIBLE.
I GOT A LOOK AT THE BODIES. UP CLOSE.
"THE VICTIMS WERE STABBED REPEATEDLY IN THE FACE AND TORSO.
"SMALL CUTS, WITHOUT MUCH STRENGTH BEHIND THEM. MOST OF THE KIDS LOOKED LIKE THEY DIED OF BLOOD LOSS."
BUT A FEW BODIES HAD OTHER CUTS ON THEM--BIG, BROAD STROKES, DONE WITH ALMOST SURGICAL ACCURACY.
WHOA. HOW'D YOU SEE ALL THAT? IS YOUR DAD A COP?
SOMETHING LIKE THAT.
MY NAME'S DAMIAN.
I'M COLIN.
AND YOU CAN CALL ME BUDDY.

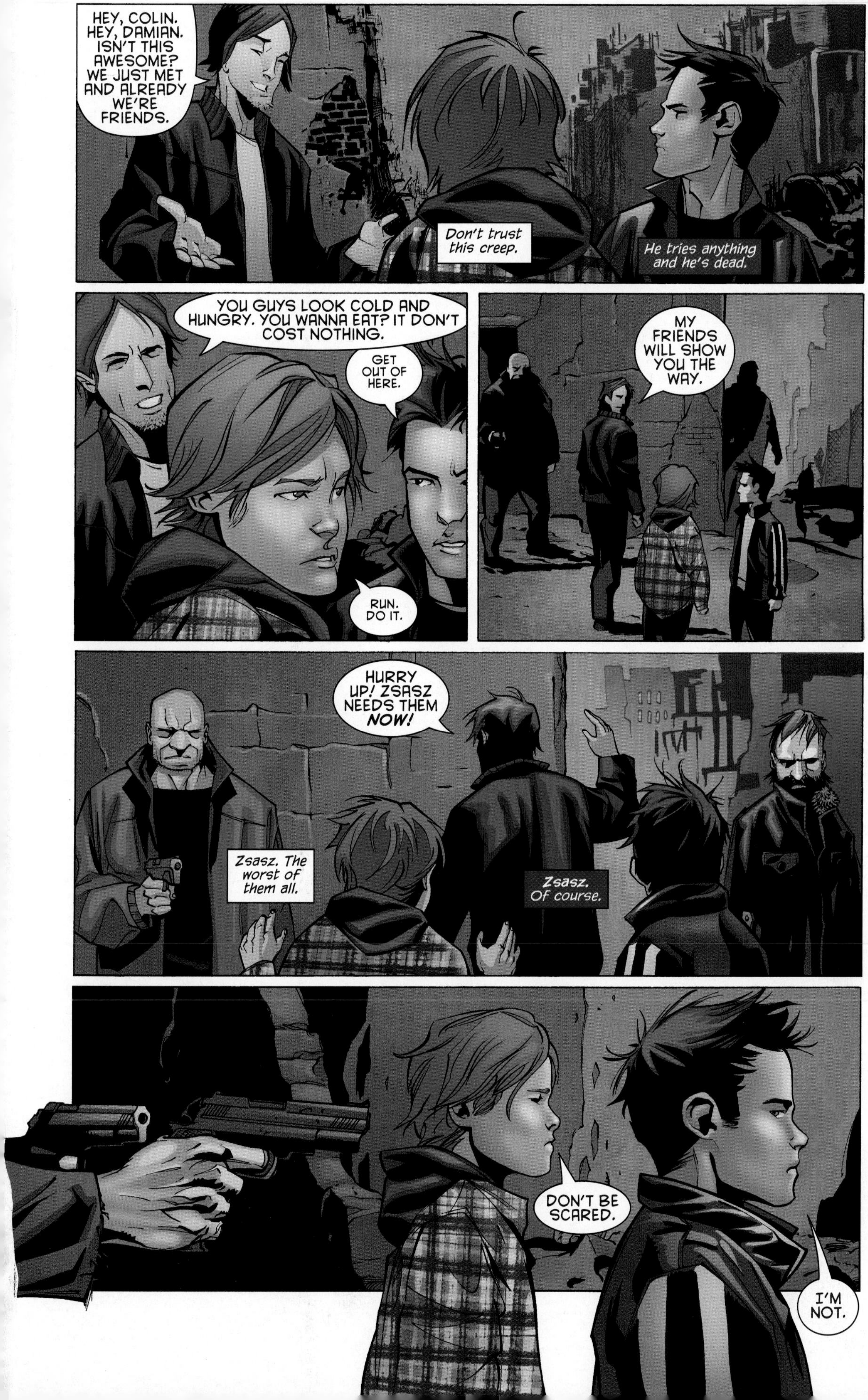
HEY, COLIN. HEY, DAMIAN. ISN'T THIS AWESOME? WE JUST MET AND ALREADY WE'RE FRIENDS.
Don't trust this creep.
He tries anything and he's dead.
YOU GUYS LOOK COLD AND HUNGRY. YOU WANNA EAT? IT DON'T COST NOTHING.
GET OUT OF HERE.
RUN. DO IT.
MY FRIENDS WILL SHOW YOU THE WAY.
HURRY UP! ZSASZ NEEDS THEM NOW!
Zsasz. The worst of them all.
Zsasz. Of course.
DON'T BE SCARED.
I'M NOT.

COME ON! GET OUT OF HERE!

I'M STAYING! I CAN HELP YOU!

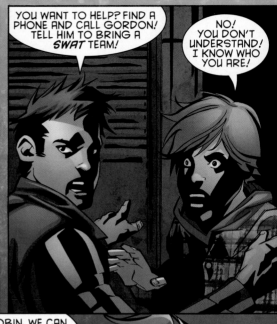

YOU WANT TO HELP? FIND A PHONE AND CALL GORDON! TELL HIM TO BRING A *SWAT* TEAM!

NO! YOU DON'T UNDERSTAND! I KNOW WHO YOU ARE!

ROBIN, WE CAN BRING DOWN ZSASZ *TOGETHER!* YOU'VE GOT TO TRUST ME!

OH, DAMN IT...

I'LL SHOW Y--

THUDD

SORRY, KID, YOU'RE OUT OF YOUR LEAGUE!

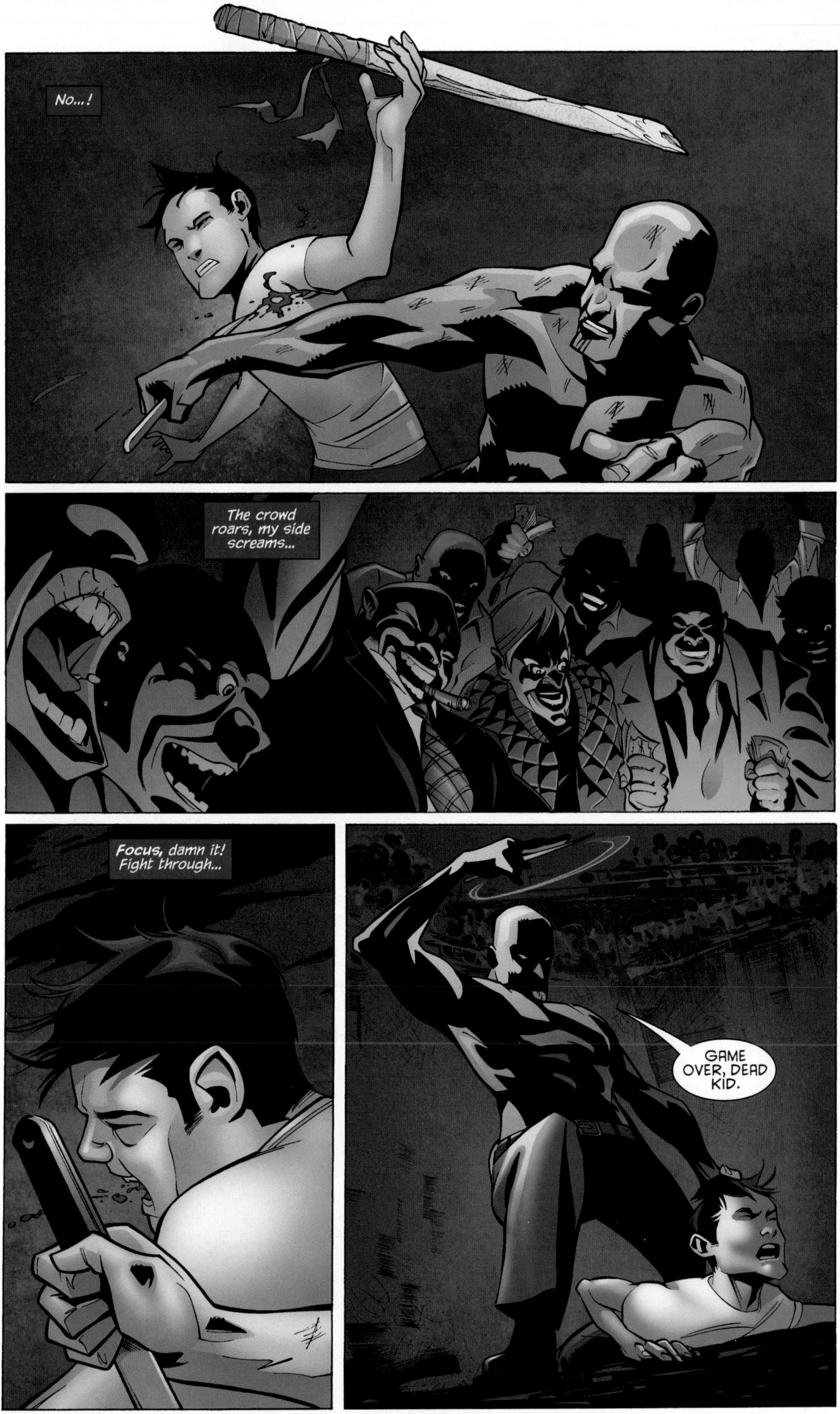
No...!
The crowd roars, my side screams...
Focus, damn it! Fight through...
GAME OVER, DEAD KID.

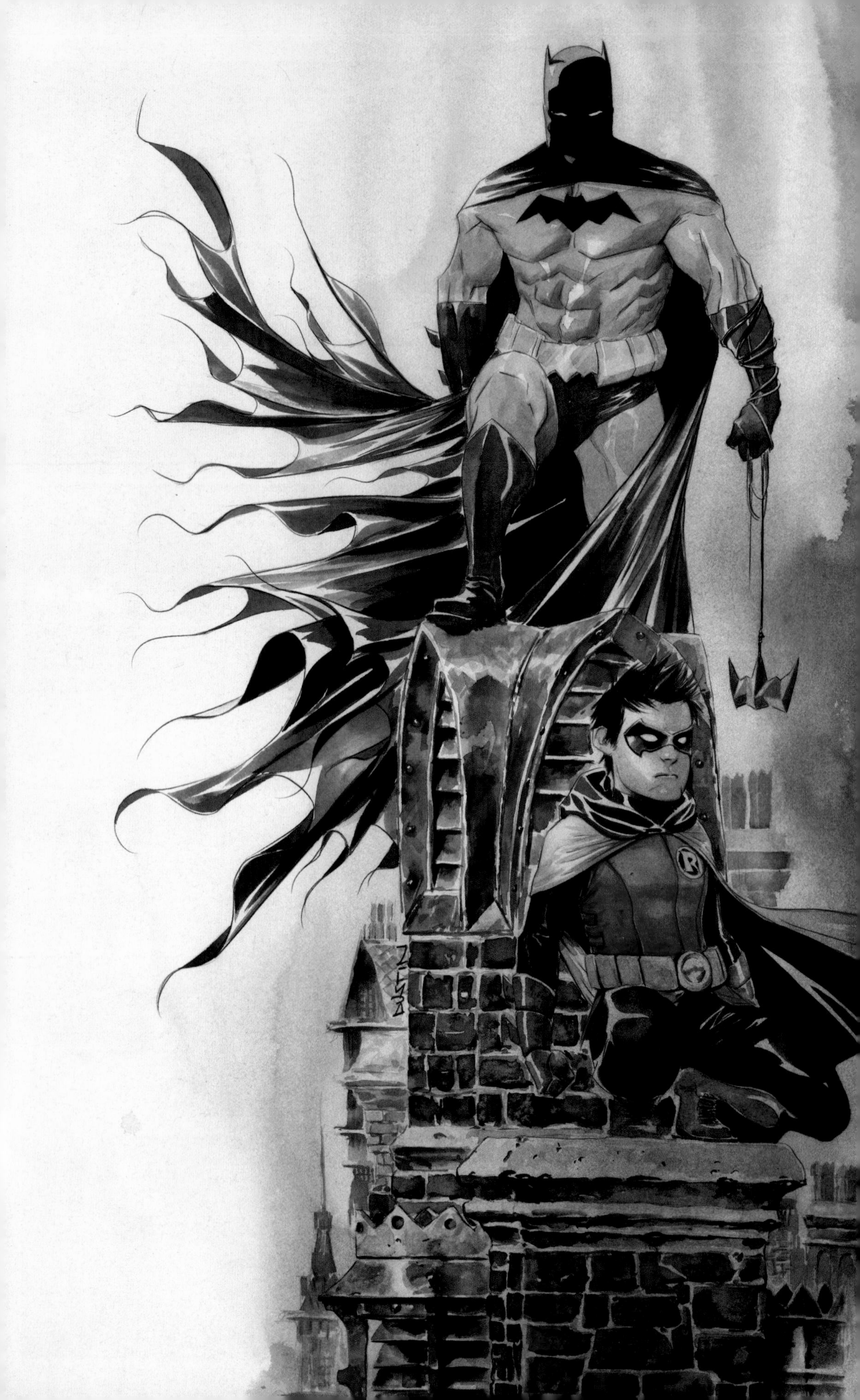

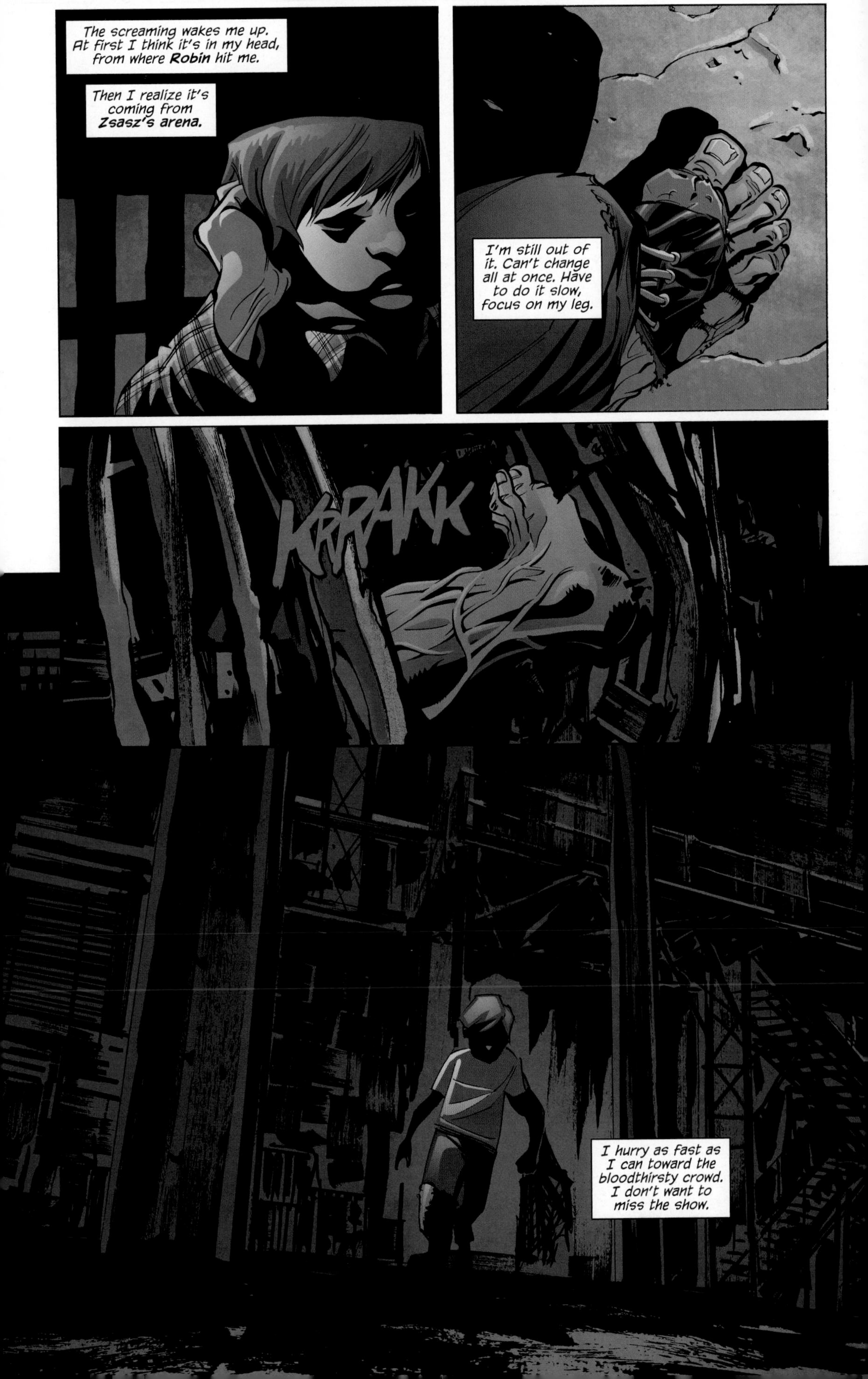
The screaming wakes me up. At first I think it's in my head, from where **Robin** hit me.
Then I realize it's coming from **Zsasz's arena.**
I'm still out of it. Can't change all at once. Have to do it slow, focus on my leg.
KRRAKK
I hurry as fast as I can toward the bloodthirsty crowd. I don't want to miss the show.

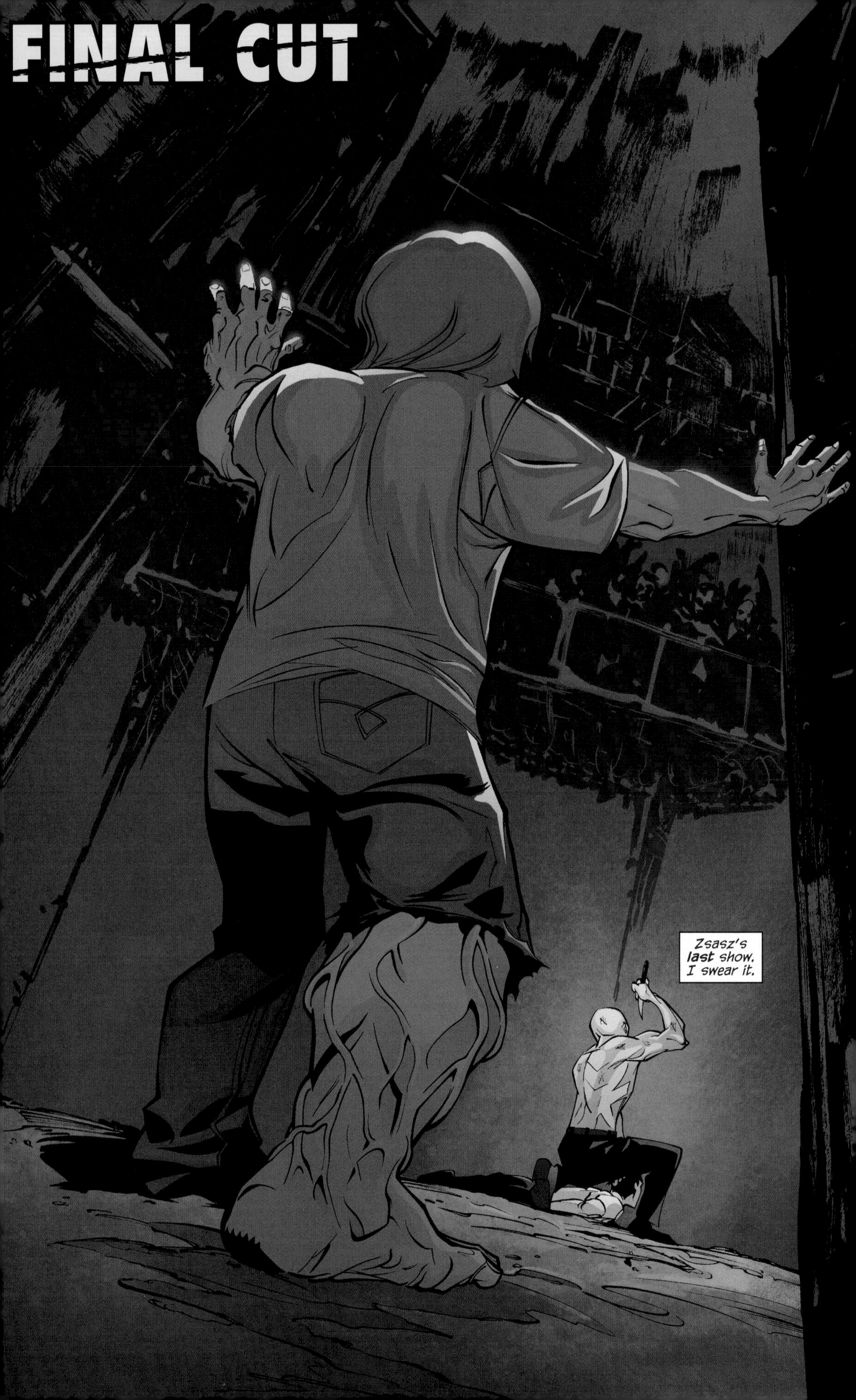
FINAL CUT
Zsasz's last show. I swear it.

144

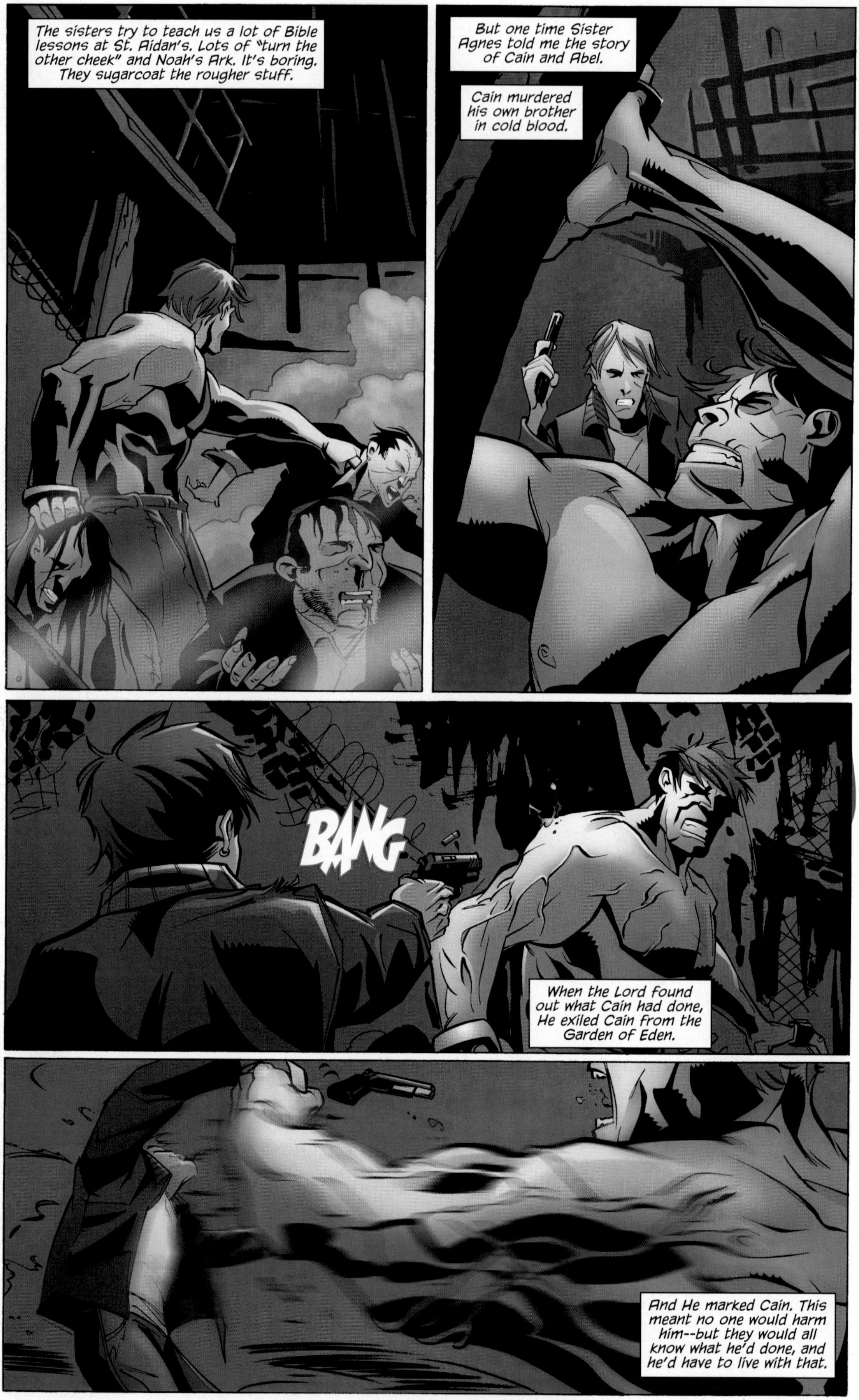
The sisters try to teach us a lot of Bible lessons at St. Aidan's. Lots of "turn the other cheek" and Noah's Ark. It's boring. They sugarcoat the rougher stuff.
But one time Sister Agnes told me the story of Cain and Abel.
Cain murdered his own brother in cold blood.
BANG
When the Lord found out what Cain had done, He exiled Cain from the Garden of Eden.
And He marked Cain. This meant no one would harm him--but they would all know what he'd done, and he'd have to live with that.

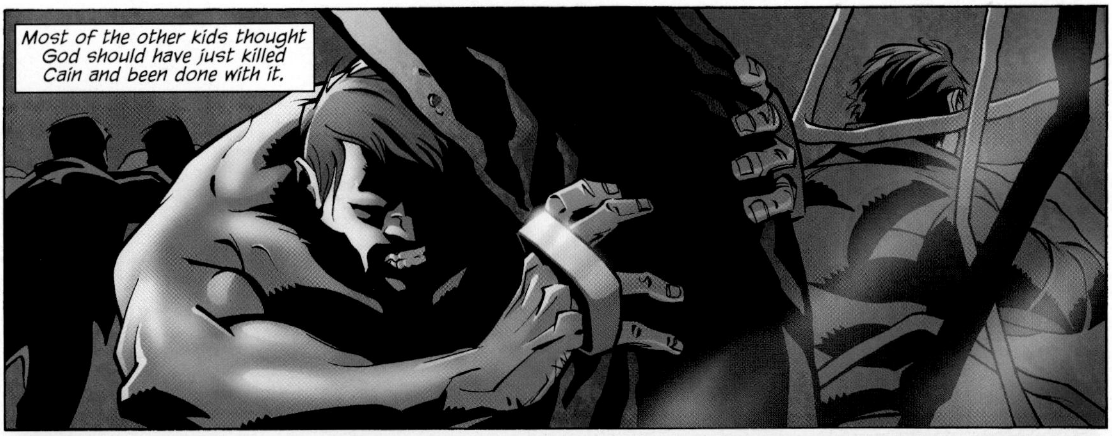
Most of the other kids thought God should have just killed Cain and been done with it.

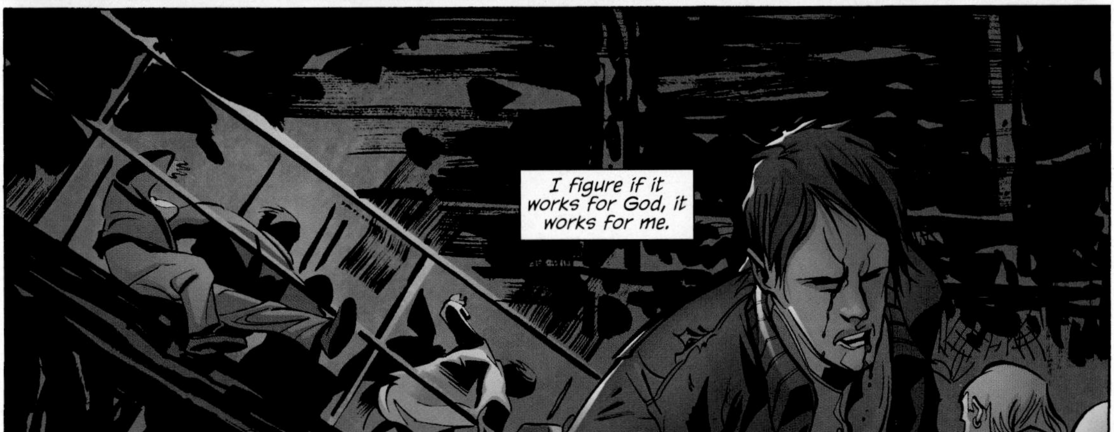
I figure if it works for God, it works for me.

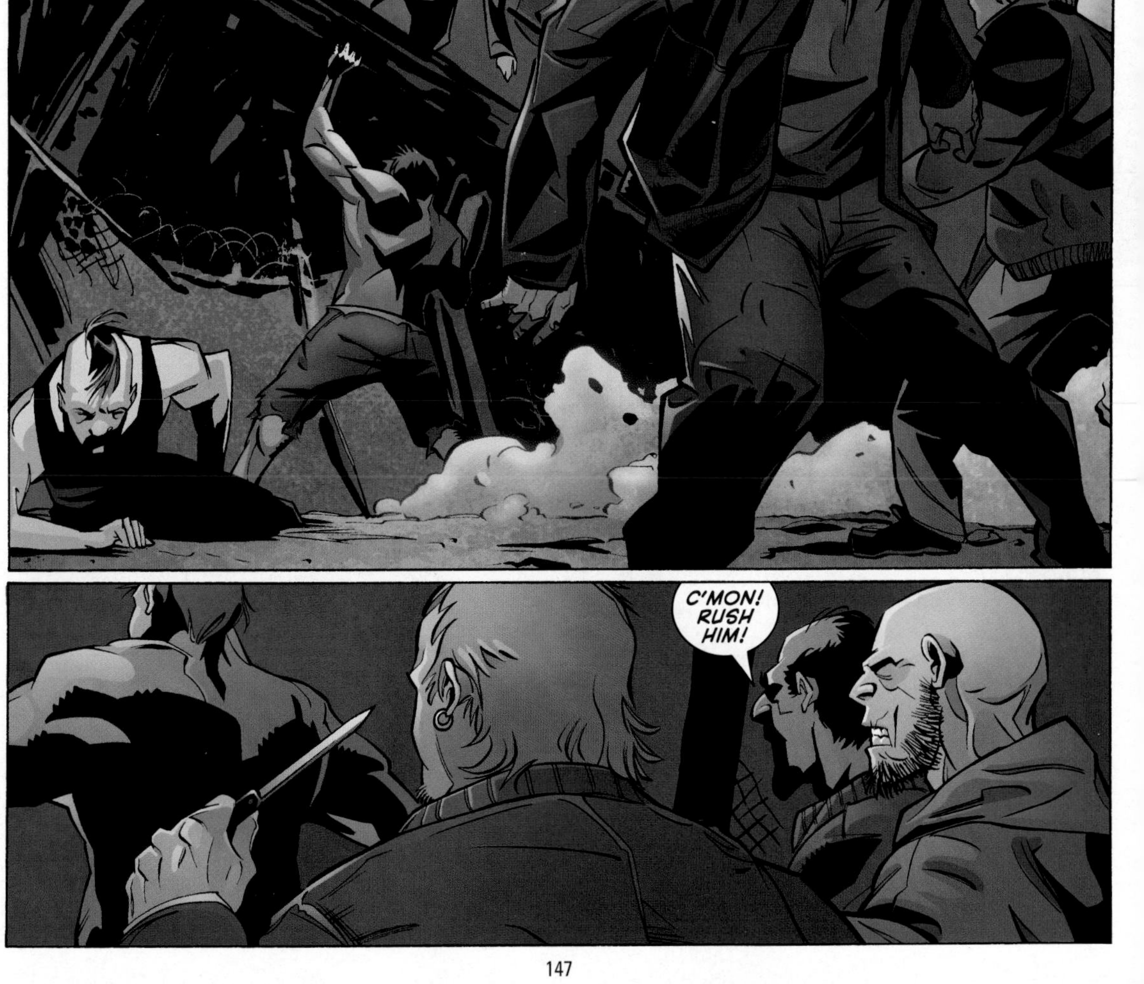
C'MON! RUSH HIM!

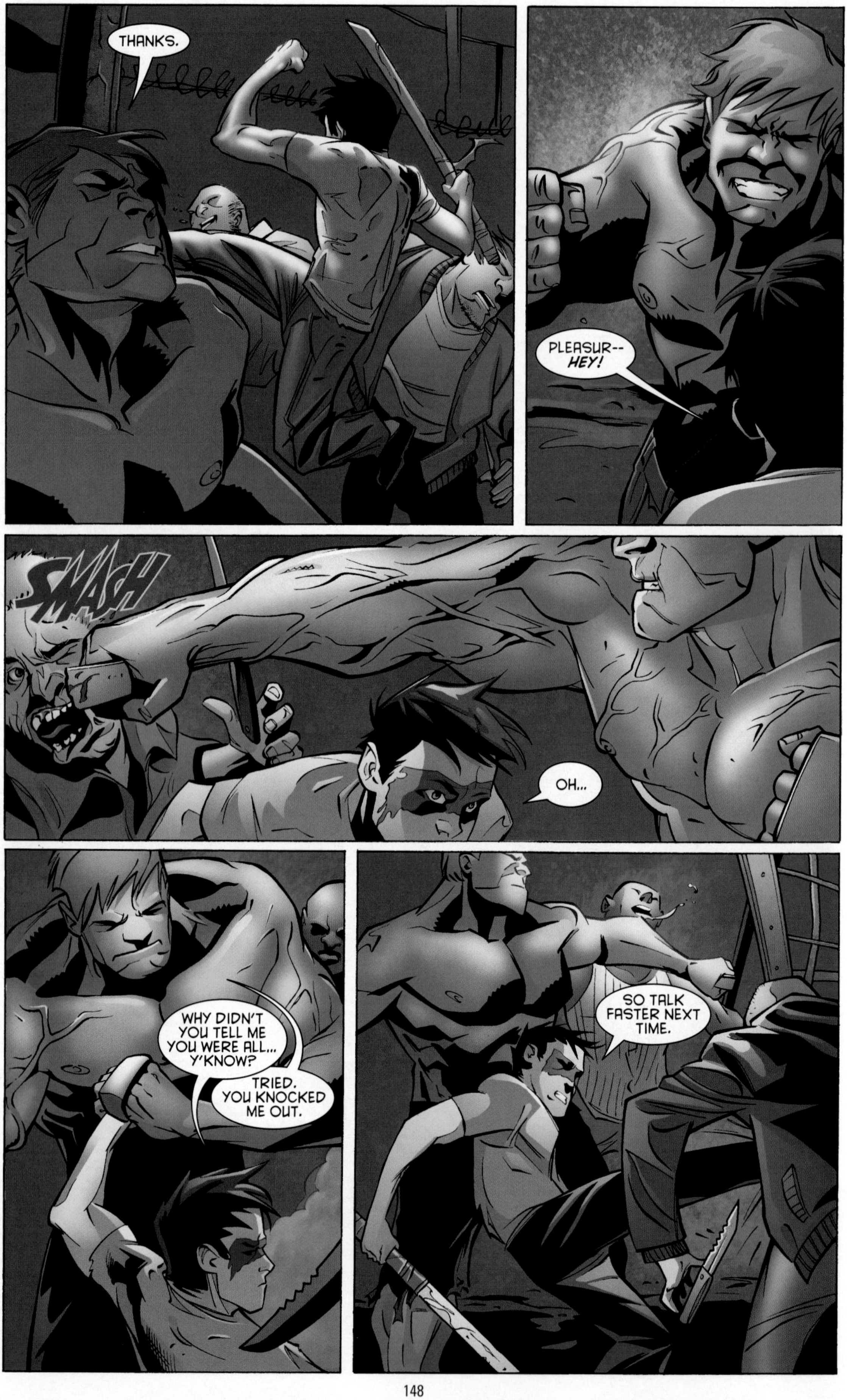
THANKS.
PLEASUR-- HEY!
SMASH
OH...
WHY DIDN'T YOU TELL ME YOU WERE ALL... Y'KNOW?
TRIED. YOU KNOCKED ME OUT.
SO TALK FASTER NEXT TIME.

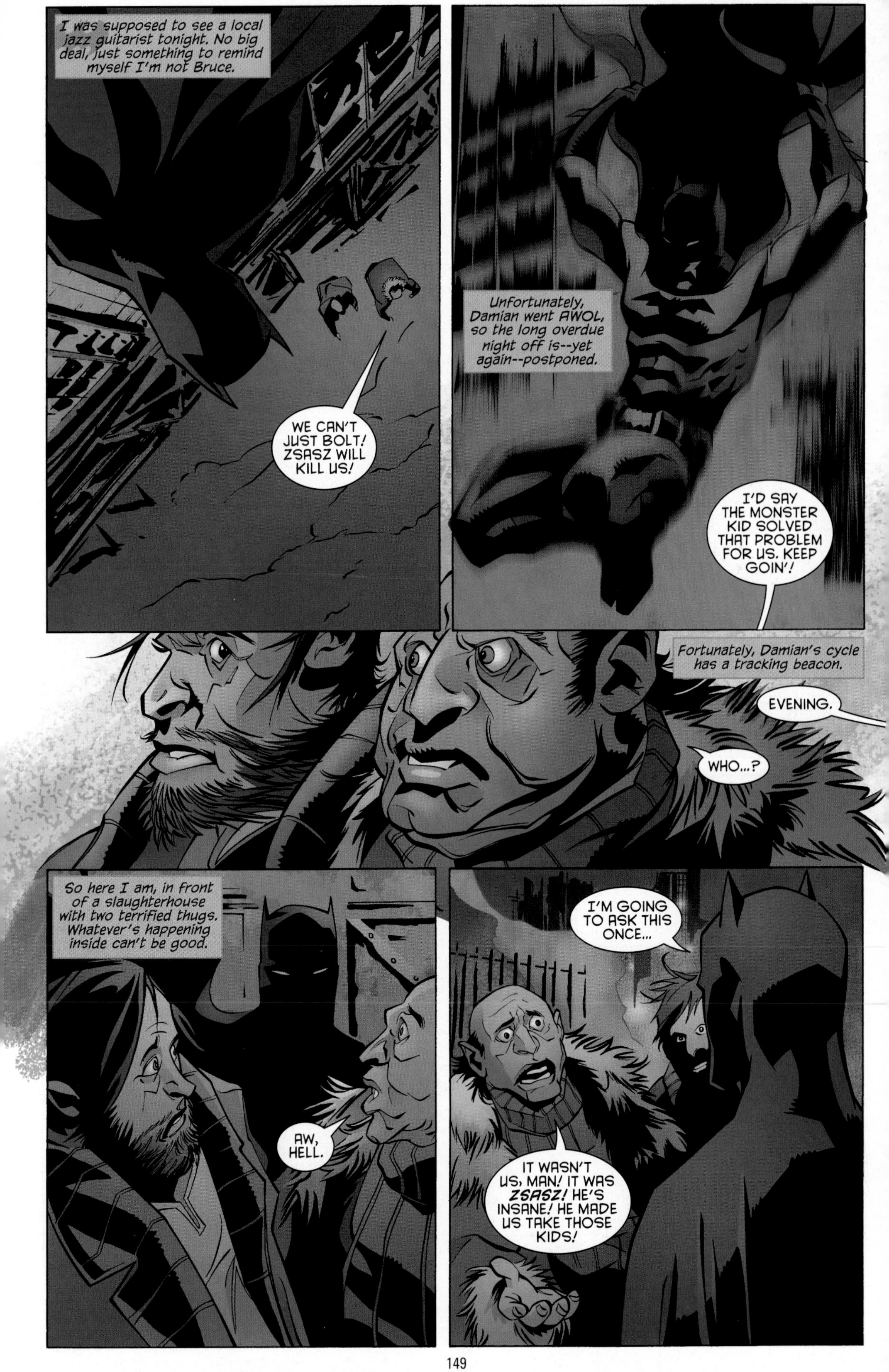
I was supposed to see a local jazz guitarist tonight. No big deal, just something to remind myself I'm not Bruce.
WE CAN'T JUST BOLT! ZSASZ WILL KILL US!
Unfortunately, Damian went AWOL, so the long overdue night off is--yet again--postponed.
I'D SAY THE MONSTER KID SOLVED THAT PROBLEM FOR US. KEEP GOIN'!
Fortunately, Damian's cycle has a tracking beacon.
EVENING.
WHO...?
So here I am, in front of a slaughterhouse with two terrified thugs. Whatever's happening inside can't be good.
AW, HELL.
I'M GOING TO ASK THIS ONCE...
IT WASN'T US, MAN! IT WAS ZSASZ! HE'S INSANE! HE MADE US TAKE THOSE KIDS!

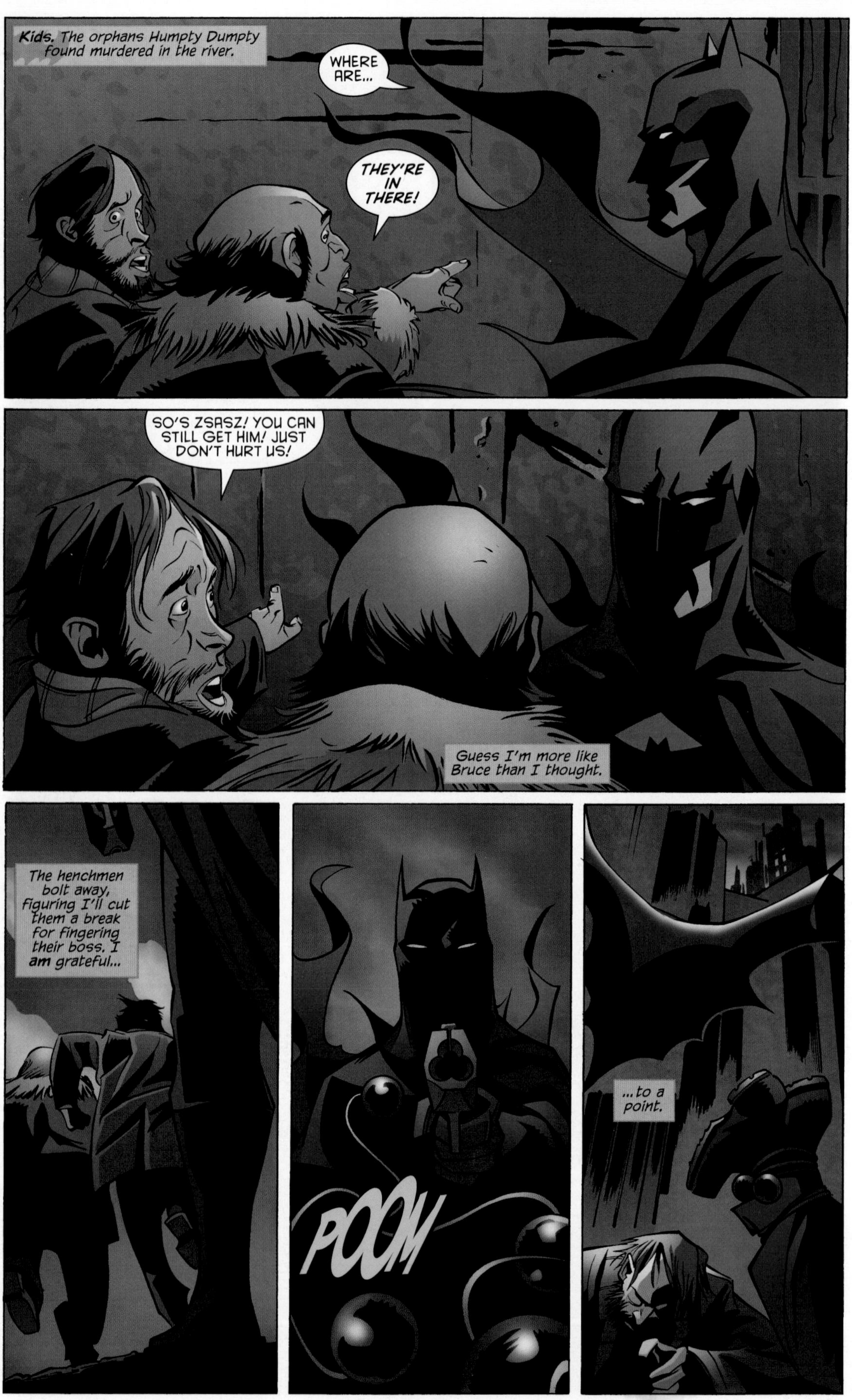

Kids. The orphans Humpty Dumpty found murdered in the river.
WHERE ARE...
THEY'RE IN THERE!
SO'S ZSASZ! YOU CAN STILL GET HIM! JUST DON'T HURT US!
Guess I'm more like Bruce than I thought.
The henchmen bolt away, figuring I'll cut them a break for fingering their boss. I am grateful...
POOM
...to a point.

I'm bleeding...

I GOT YA, MR. ZSASZ. IT'S ME--BUDDY.

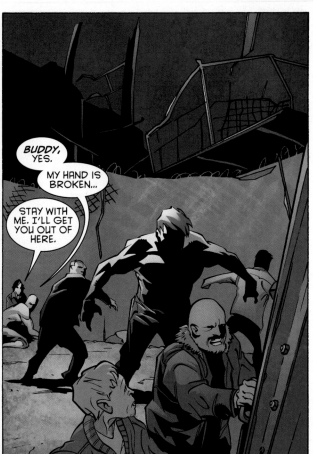

BUDDY, YES.

MY HAND IS BROKEN...

STAY WITH ME. I'LL GET YOU OUT OF HERE.

THAT THING, THAT *MONSTER!* HE'S RUINED ME!

I'll see him *dead* for this, him and that other kid!

I'LL DANCE IN THEIR BLOOD...

BOSS! YOU DON'T STAND A CHANCE! HE'S A FREAK!

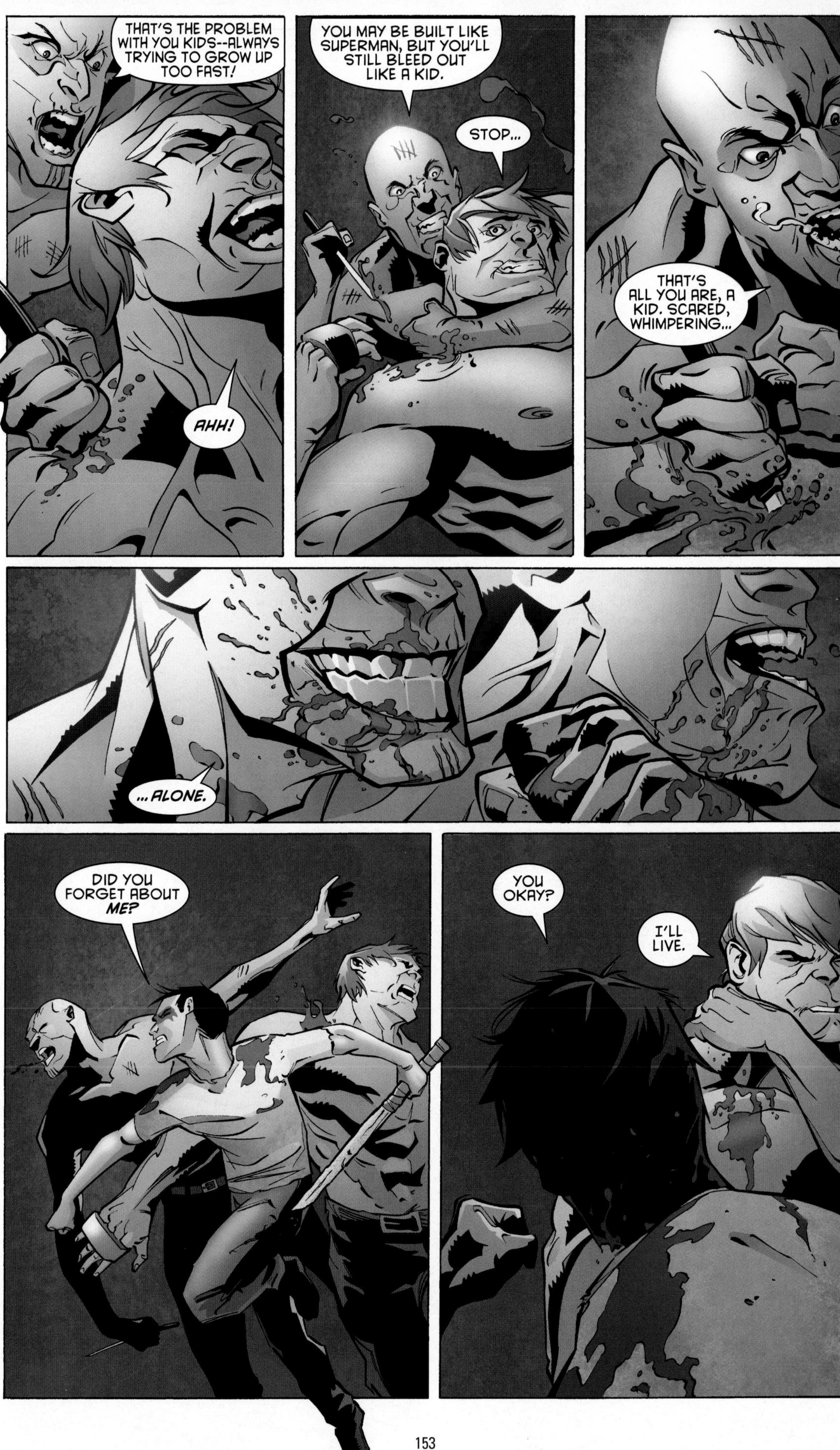
THAT'S THE PROBLEM WITH YOU KIDS--ALWAYS TRYING TO GROW UP TOO FAST!
AHH!
YOU MAY BE BUILT LIKE SUPERMAN, BUT YOU'LL STILL BLEED OUT LIKE A KID.
STOP...
THAT'S ALL YOU ARE, A KID. SCARED, WHIMPERING...
...ALONE.
DID YOU FORGET ABOUT ME?
YOU OKAY?
I'LL LIVE.

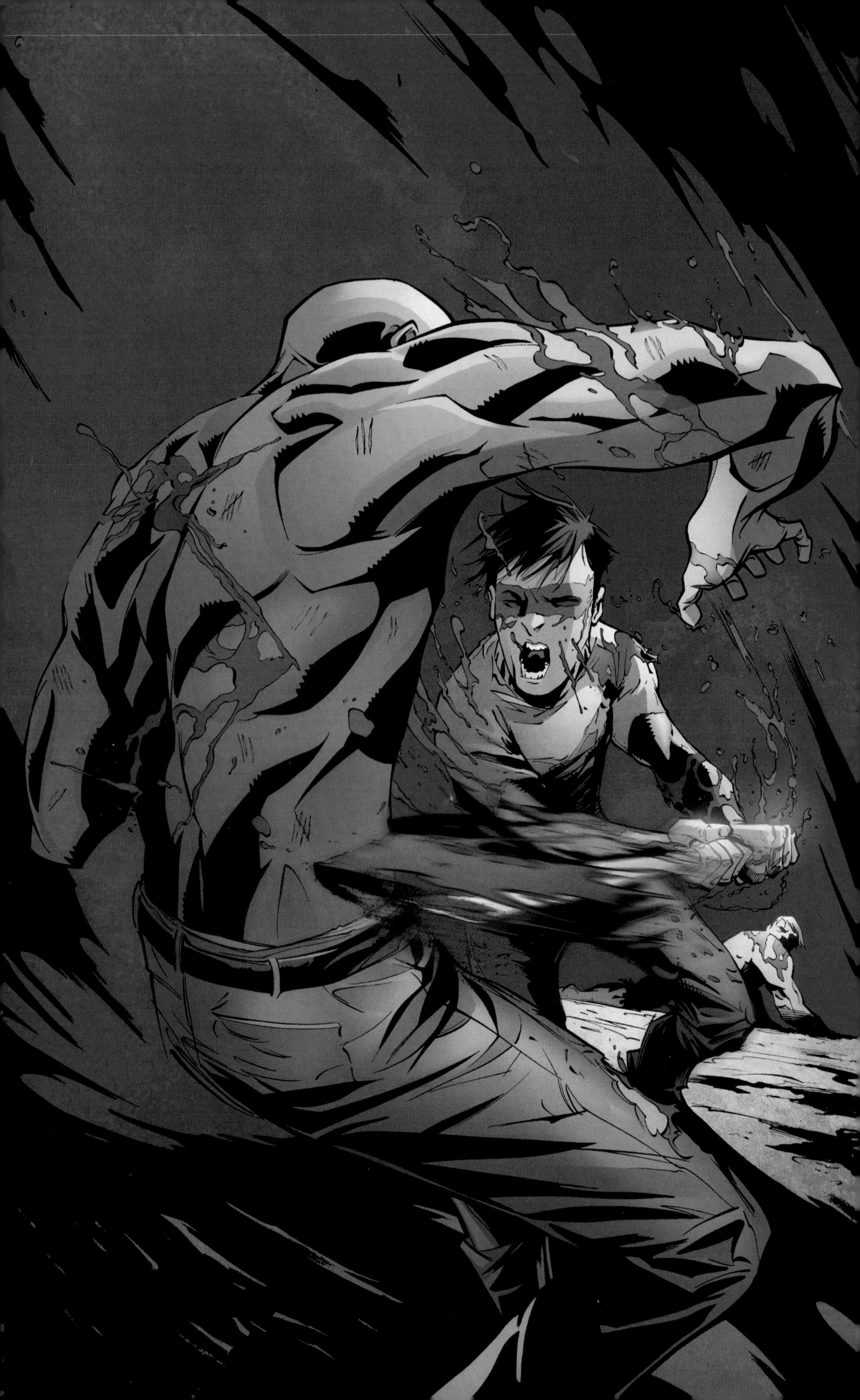

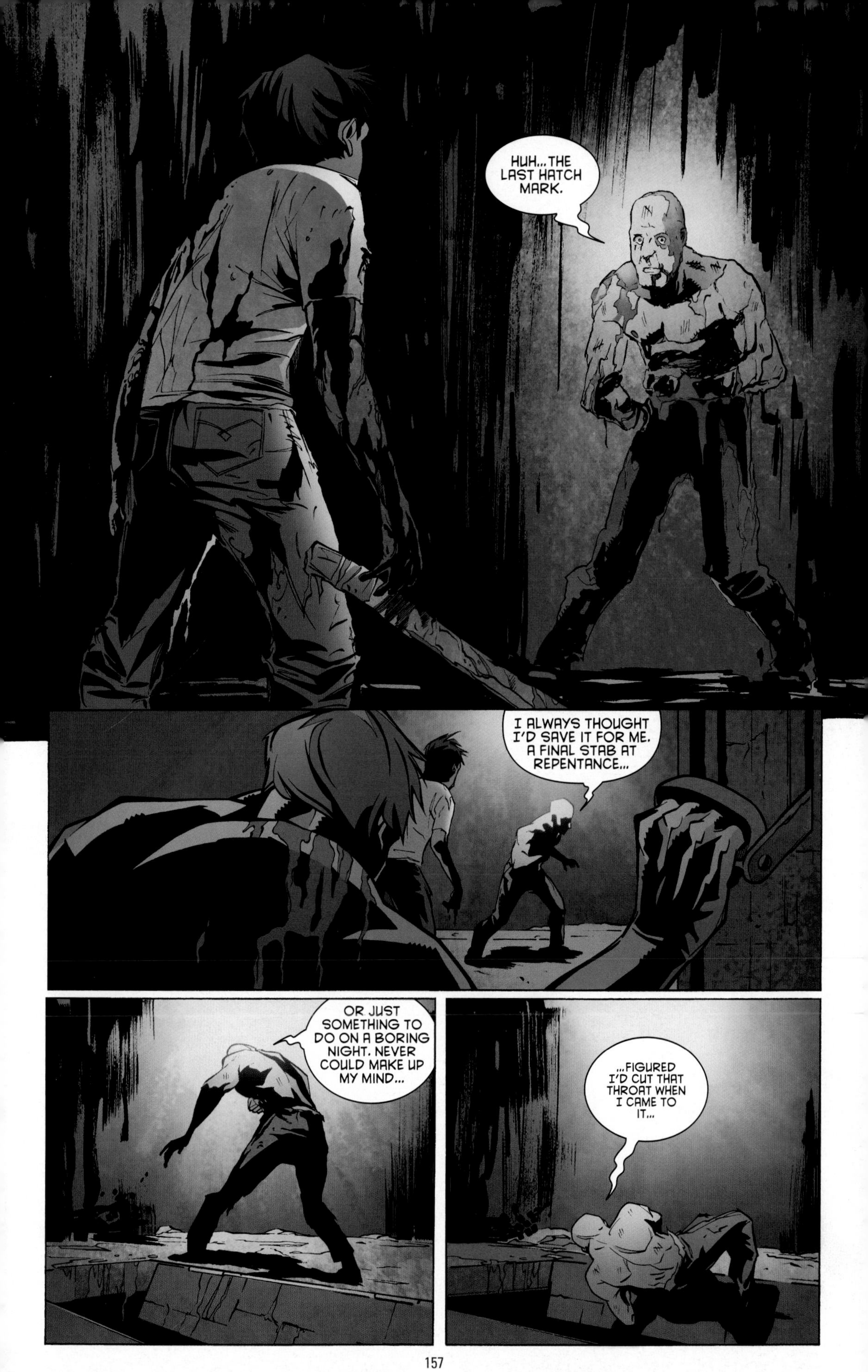
HUH... THE LAST HATCH MARK.
I ALWAYS THOUGHT I'D SAVE IT FOR ME. A FINAL STAB AT REPENTANCE...
OR JUST SOMETHING TO DO ON A BORING NIGHT. NEVER COULD MAKE UP MY MIND...
...FIGURED I'D CUT THAT THROAT WHEN I CAME TO IT...